Trea$ure Your Life

A True Story

by

- Cher Lindberg

Wilshire Press, Inc.

Trea$ure Your Life

Copyright © 2013
Revised 4-14-2014
Cher Lee Lindberg

All rights reserved. No part of this book may be used or reproduced by any means, graphic, electronic, or mechanical, including photocopying, recording, taping or by any information storage retrieval system without the written permission of the author except in the case of brief quotations embodied in critical articles and reviews.

To contact the author, write to
Cher Lindberg, PO Box 141468, Minneapolis, MN 55414

email: cher@TreasureYourLife.com
website: www.TreasureYourLife.com

This book may be ordered from the online Bookstore at The Book Patch

Title: Trea$ure Your Life at www.TheBookPatch.com

Because of the dynamic nature of the Internet, any web addresses or links contained in this book may have changed since publication and may no longer be valid. The views expressed in this work are solely those of the author and do not necessarily reflect the views of the publisher, and the publisher hereby disclaims any responsibility for them.

Grateful acknowledgement is made for permission to reprint paragraphs from the following copyrighted works: "The Smartest Guys in the Room"
by Bethany McLean and Peter Elkind,
© 2003, 10 year Edition © 2013

Cover design: Belinda Kveen,
Kveen Design LLC

ISBN 978-1-6203-0827-1 (sc)

Printed in the United States of America

Wilshire Press, Inc.

Dedication:

This book is dedicated to my mother Doris who always believed in me.

To my 2nd mother Dee who inspired me to push beyond my limits.

To my Grandma Mabel Lindberg and my Uncle Larry Lindberg, who both left us way too soon and my nephew Bob Lindberg who is still with us.

To my Dad, Lee Lindberg, who has been there as a source of guidance for me.

To Sarah, who has kept me alive all these years by being my Daughter.

Finally to my good friend Sheridan who gave me something to do in order to save my own Life.

Acknowledgements:

As with any endeavor, acknowledgements are important to the success of any project.

I want thank my friend Lauri Flaquer who I met several years ago at the Woman's Club in Minneapolis. She pushed me to finish this book more than anyone else. Her marketing insight and creative ideas helped me during the times I was emotionally stuck and unable to go on.

I want to thank my friend Deb Callahan, who encouraged me and stood by me many times when I felt overwhelmed. She even helped me get my own website up: www.TreasureYourLife.com

I want to thank my Irondale High School friend, Sally (Hogquist) Nelson who has been there for me since high school and encouraged me to keep going during the book writing process. She is still married to my next-door Neighbor who I grew up with. Greg.

Thanks to my Prospect Park friend, Lori Schletty, who helped me through some difficult emotional times dealing with my layoff. She has been an outstanding mentor and life coach as she encouraged me to continue with the book.

I want to thank my reviewers who gave me positive feedback on this book as I was writing it: Mike Hedman, Gay Lynn Neitzel, Dana Thielen, Lee Lindberg, Gayle Herwig, and Grace Lindberg.

Special thanks to my daughter Sarah who spent time to do her magic on the final drafts of the book, creating the Table of Contents and formatting files for the final copy. Plus creating numerous pdf versions of the book for me. Like a child, you are never done with it. The book I mean.

Unexpected thanks to a young woman I met in the pool at LA Fitness, Belinda Kveen, who is the same age as my daughter Sarah and who agreed to take on the cover design of this book. It was her first book cover after doing other graphic design projects. Graphics is one of her passions. This wasn't even her day 'job'. I think she did a great job!

Thanks to a wise man, Cornbread Harris (James Samuel Harris, Sr.) who proofread the manuscript on 8 ½ - 11 inch paper and came up with a quote on the back cover that tied all the things together I was trying to say. He's a kind heart from the old school.

Special thanks to another Irondale High School friend of mine, Janine Timm, one of my first editors on the project who came up with a list of minor corrections that nobody else saw, including me. She created a quote for the back cover, too. Her dad, Marv and my dad, Lee were close friends while we were growing up in New Brighton. She also went through a devastating layoff from her place of employment after 30 years. She could relate to the emotional experience of what I went through.

I want to thank and acknowledge the Women of Unity from my Golden Valley church who have supported and encouraged me to not only finish writing this book but to publish it. They have been a tremendous source of support!!

Finally, to my friend Sheridan, who still hasn't read the book but who encouraged me to finish it.

There are many more people in my life to thank, but for now this is it.

Thank God!
-Cher

Table of Contents

Introduction 1
Chapter 1 ~ Life or Death 3
Chapter 2 ~ The Decision 37
Chapter 3 ~ The Dragonfly 58
Chapter 4 ~ The Argument 98
Chapter 5 ~ Discovering Tree Frogs 109
Chapter 6 ~ Setting a Goal 120
Chapter 7 ~ Finding Mentone 130
Chapter 8 ~ The Donkey 139
Chapter 9 ~ The Blessing 153
Chapter 10 ~ Playing with Fire 167
Chapter 11 ~ Staying in Mentone? 174
Chapter 12 ~ Learning to Live 187
Chapter 13 ~ Leaving Mentone 207
ENDNOTES 241

Introduction

This is a **true story** of my journey from a sudden and unexpected layoff to a realization after 8 years that I felt worthless, life was hopeless, my house was a mess and nobody wanted me.

I hit bottom and bounced back realizing that if I could come back to appreciate Life, so could others. I almost did myself in and planned to end my life one afternoon on July 15th and through reasons I can't explain I didn't do anything.

Except change my thoughts.

Thoughts are powerful. Thoughts become words. Words become actions. Actions create a sense of accomplishment.

And a sense of accomplishment can change the world.

One Baby Step at a time.

Some names in the story have been changed. All events and people are real. I'm not creative enough to make this stuff up.

-Cher Lindberg
Minneapolis, Minnesota
December 2013

Chapter 1 ~ Life or Death

It was 4:30 pm, Friday, July 15th. Cheryl's husband had been gone for 3 hours. He was on his way up north to a Minnesota cabin for a Guys Weekend.

Cheryl was looking forward to having the house to herself so she could clean and throw things away. Her husband was a Packrat. He didn't throw anything out. He even gave Cheryl a hard time when she threw her own things out. It was one of their problems. He kept stuff and she didn't.

Cheryl called Michael the King of the Packrats.

With him gone she could toss whatever she wanted without him saying anything. By the time he got back from his Guys Weekend the house would be clean ~ except for Michael's living room. It was full of newspapers. Boxes and piles of them. Everywhere. On his couch. Behind his living room chair. On the floor. Behind the bookcases. Newspapers stacked on top of newspapers.

There was no place to sit in *his* living room.

The newspapers had a musty smell. Not a bad one, just an old dusty one. There was no escaping it. It was definitely in the air.

They had *his* and *her* living rooms in the 106 year old house located in Prospect Park. The oldest neighborhood in the heart of Minneapolis. The neighborhood was home to the Witch's Hat Water Tower built in 1913 and looking like a witch's hat with a pointed top. On a hill overlooking the city of Minneapolis and close to their house. It was one of the few original water towers of that era still standing.

Both of them suffered during their 1st marriages arguing with spouses over shared spaces. Having separate living rooms right off the bat was the only way they could maintain their sanity. They each made the rules for their own living rooms.

Looking around at the chaotic mess that now existed in BOTH living rooms only 3 hours after Michael left for the weekend, Cheryl realized her Master Cleaning Plan had not gone well.

She was suddenly faced with ending her own life.

The mess in every room of the house combined with the fact she didn't have a job was overwhelming.

I just want to give up. I feel worthless.

Cheryl looked around at the clutter in her own living room. She saw junk mail, unpaid bills, papers piled high on her coffee table, clothes in a suitcase she hadn't unpacked from her last trip to Chicago, her bathrobe, a bamboo plant dying in front of her and other indications of neglect.

As she looked at the chaos, she thought, "This isn't working! I want out of here. Not just out of this place but out of this LIFE!!"

These thoughts ran threw her mind after her Bally's fitness center partner left – a guy named Sheridan. She had invited him to come over as soon as Michael was gone. Her goal was to have Sheridan give her advice on where to start in the house. She knew Sheridan loved to clean and organize.

It was an effort that ended in total disaster.

Sheridan came over promptly at 2 pm. Cheryl showed him around the house and asked him where she should start cleaning: upstairs at her desk, downstairs in the kitchen, her living room, the bathroom, anyplace.

After surveying the total chaos Sheridan said calmly, "I think the best place to start cleaning would be the sun porch."

His reasoning was that if she could eliminate the clutter from the sun porch it would become usable again. Cheryl could have a place of refuge while she cleaned other areas of the house.

It sounded like a good plan. Sheridan attempted to help her get started. But once they both decided on the sun porch as an attack plan, everything he suggested met with resistance from Cheryl.

"No, I can't move that because it's Michael's stuff. He'll get mad."

or

"I don't know where to put that."

After 2 hours of trying to help her, Sheridan lost his temper.

"This place is TOTAL CHAOS!! It's a COCK BLOCK!!! No WONDER Michael doesn't find you sexually attractive anymore!! It's a complete mess around here!!!"

Cheryl was shocked! She started crying.

"What!!?"

She was trying to comprehend what he said. Her thoughts were racing.

TREA$URE YOUR LIFE | 5

In her mind, she said to herself, "I've never heard that phrase in my entire life!! What does it mean??? A cock block??? What!??"

She could only imagine it had something to do with her sex life. But her sex life with Michael was NOT something she discussed with Sheridan on their 5 am workouts at the Bally's club every morning. She was confused. She thought the sex life in her marriage was fine.

"Sher," (← that's what she called him), "I brought you over here to help me get started. NOT to yell at me!! You knew it was a mess before you came over. I was counting on you to help me get organized!!"

Cheryl's mind raced back 2 years before when Sheridan made a tremendous impact on her house after a kitchen fire. It was a fire Cheryl accidentally started by forgetting to turn a burner off on top of the stove. She was heating up leftovers. She remembered grabbing the leftovers in the frying pan off the stove but forgot about the burner.

She had returned exhausted that night after giving piano lessons to her students in the western suburbs of Minneapolis near Lake Minnetonka.

She fell asleep during the Jay Leno monologue that night while eating her leftovers and then woke up shortly afterwards to numbly walk up the stairs. Her husband Michael joined her in the bedroom. He had been working upstairs in his office the whole time. He was a Webmaster and was always under a deadline to get a client's web site up and running.

As they both drifted off to sleep, the house filled with smoke. The smoke detectors in the house did not have batteries in them anymore. The unattended hot burner downstairs melted a plastic cup located 2 inches away from it. The melting plastic from the cup slowly crept onto the burner and then burst into flames.

The plastic cup was one of her favorites. It was from a Superbowl football game at the Dome in Minneapolis, several years before. The only Superbowl that had ever been played in Minneapolis. The only game where her daughter Sarah danced in the half time show as part of the event and Cheryl was there to see it in person.

A rare cup, for sure.

Michael woke up that night in a panic saying, "I smell SMOKE! ELECTRICAL AND PLASTIC SMOKE!!"

He raced down the stairs and grabbed the fire extinguisher located near the door of the kitchen. Cheryl stumbled down in time to see Michael putting out high flames on top of the stove with a lot of white powder from the fire extinguisher being sprayed EVERYWHERE.

It had a dramatic negative effect on their relationship. Michael screamed at the top of his lungs that night saying things Cheryl would never forget.

"HOW COULD YOU DO THIS!!!! DON'T YOU KNOW THIS HOUSE IS THE MOST PRECIOUS THING I HAVE??? IT'S MY CASTLE!!! IT'S THE ONLY THING I HAVE TO PROVE THAT I'M NOT POOR!!! IT'S THE ONE THING THAT HAS SURVIVED ME AND MY PREVIOUS MARRIAGE!!!"

Michael left 2 days later in March of that year to visit his mother in Austin, Texas. His trip to Texas was an event that occurred every year during their marriage. Cheryl rarely accompanied him to visit his mother.

It was while Michael was gone for 3 weeks two years before that Cheryl discovered Sheridan's passion for cleaning. He was an absolute workhorse!!

Sheridan came back to her house every morning after their 5 am workouts to help her clean up the black smoke mess from the fire. He loved cleaning. He tackled areas of the kitchen that Cheryl would NEVER have cleaned. Cheryl started calling him 'Mr. Clean'.

He sanded the countertops. He vacuumed the high ceiling where the smoke attached itself to spider webs she had never noticed. It looked as if someone sprayed black silly string everywhere on the ceiling.

He cleaned the outside of the kitchen cupboards. He washed all the dishes and glasses that were inside the cupboards and still covered in black smoke from the fire. The black smoke went everywhere. It had no boundaries. Not even closed cupboards. It was like a ghost. A black one.

The more he cleaned the more they both got energized.

Not only did they get stuff done they had *fun* while cleaning. They had music on and danced while they cleaned. They came up with a new way of eating carrots while dancing and cleaning. They actually *laughed*!

Who would have thought cleaning up a black smoke mess from a fire could be fun? It was a dreadful project that they managed to turn into a memorable event.

Cheryl did *not* do that with anybody else. Not cleaning the house. Cleaning was *not* one of her favorite activities.

Cheryl and Sheridan were unemployed during the 3 weeks Michael was gone so they spent entire days cleaning her and Michael's house. By the time Michael got back from his trip to Texas, almost all traces of the black smoke were gone.

That is why 2 years after the fire, Sheridan was Cheryl's last hope in helping her clean the house. If HE couldn't figure out how to get her started cleaning, nobody could.

She asked Sheridan only for some help getting started. A 2-hour commitment from him was what she needed to launch herself into a cleaning machine. Or tornado. Whatever worked.

As Sheridan was leaving in exasperation at 4:30 pm to go swimming at Bally's with his Friday night swimming partner on July 15, he stopped and gave her one last look.

She was still sobbing. He had *never* seen her cry before.

"You know, Cher," (← that's what he called her) "if you want I could come back and check on you in 2 hours. Just do something – ANYTHING and you'll feel better. Do you want me to check back on you??"

"OK." Cheryl mumbled through her tears. "If you want to."

She hadn't expected him to come back. That was not part of her original Master Cleaning Plan.

After Sheridan left, Cheryl started thinking about the shocking phrase Sheridan said to her. Now she wasn't even sexy anymore to her own husband???

TREA$URE YOUR LIFE | 9

She thought about how her life might have been different. She had one of those internal conversations with herself while she tried to analyze the situation.

"IF ONLY I had married Lee after my first divorce when I had the chance. We were young and 20-somethings. He was the first love for me after I divorced my high school sweetheart, John.

What was I thinking??! Lee had a beautiful house in Wayzata. He bought that house because I liked it after he got divorced. He loved me. He was successful and good-looking. He looked like Tom Selleck. Incredibly handsome. Almost too much."

Her mind switched to a third person view. She started analyzing the situation from outside herself.

Everything in Lee's house was clean. He even steam cleaned the white carpets in his upstairs bedroom. He had a sailboat on Lake Minnetonka that they loved being on with their young children from first marriages.

They each had one child.

Both children were the same age when they met on a snowy day in November. Two months after Cheryl's divorce. At a classy bar and restaurant called Steak & Ale in Roseville, Minnesota. A bar that no longer existed.

Their kids were 2 years old and 2 months apart. One born in March, the other in May. Of the same year.

But after 5 years with Lee, he started going out on Cheryl behind her back.

"IF ONLY he hadn't gotten that OTHER woman pregnant during our relationship!! I trusted him. I believed him when he said he wasn't sleeping with anybody. He told me the other woman in his life was 'strictly platonic'. And that I was the love of his life."

"What about the time I got pregnant with his child??"

"I was naïve back then. He got someone pregnant he met at a bar. She was easy. Nobody ever paid attention to her that had his looks and money. She knew she'd never have anybody like him again in her life."

"What was I thinking???? Why didn't I force the marriage issue when I had the chance??!! The other woman did!"

"Because I loved him, that's why."

Lee spent the entire night before he got married to the other woman with Cheryl. He left that morning in February saying to Cheryl, "Goodbye Sweetie."

Cheryl remembered asking him as he stood in her bedroom doorway looking at her, "Lee, are you getting married today?"

He replied as he leaned his long frame against the doorway, "No, I am not."

He looked just like the cowboy drawing from the Leaning Post bar where he met the other woman. Long and lanky. A dark image against the dim light of the hallway. Leaning comfortably in his manhood with his arms folded. Good-looking even in the shadows.

But he got married that day anyway.

She thought about that part of her life as she was contemplating ending her own life. She remembered how devastated she was after Lee got married. How could he do that??? They were practically living together in his house in Wayzata!

If she had married Lee when she'd had the *chance* because they had a wedding date set, at least she wouldn't be faced with a house full of newspapers.

Ready to end her life.

She moved on and met an Architect named Bill.

"IF ONLY I had married Bill. I should have given him more time. I only gave him 5 years to make up his mind. I should have given him 6."

Bill was the only person who was able to take her attention away from Lee. Bill was smart, confident, attractive and an excellent downhill skier. He got along very well with her 7 year old daughter Sarah, even though Bill had never been married and had no children. His parents adored Sarah and also grew to love Cheryl.

She remembered how she flew out to Vail every year of her 5-year relationship with Bill and his entire family. His parents were Bob and Kitty. Kitty? Yes, that was her nickname. Included every year were Bill's brother John, his wife Kay, their kids and friends. They rented houses in Vail and shared cooking experiences as a group.

Each couple took turns cooking a dinner for everybody. Everybody skied all day. Sarah became quite good at skiing as a young girl. She was fearless going down the black diamond ski hills of Vail.

These thoughts ran threw her mind on July 15.

After 5 years of a wonderful relationship, she forced the issue with Bill. Marriage? Or not? Bill couldn't commit. He was an Architect of million dollar homes and he was married to his drawing board. He loved designing houses. He was good at it.

She finally broke up with Bill because he wouldn't marry her. She gave him an entire summer to think about it. From the 4th of July to Labor Day weekend.

Cheryl gave Bill a goodbye card on his birthday in October. That was the end of their relationship. Or so she thought.

Cheryl remembered how a few months after Bill's birthday in October she met a guy in the hot tub at US Swim & Fitness (which later became Bally's) who's nickname was Mac. They fell in love with each other almost instantly and quickly became engaged.

Both of them were in AA and had stopped drinking. It was unusual for Cheryl to meet a man who didn't drink. She had met both Lee and Bill in trendy bars.

It was a short story that had an unhappy ending. After they became engaged and Mac bought her an expensive diamond ring they decided on a wedding date of September 8.

Plans changed when Cheryl found out he was going out behind her back with his previous girlfriend. They were getting ready to order formal wedding invitations when 'The Call' happened.

Margaret called one afternoon in July while Cheryl was in the kitchen at Mac's house in Shoreview on Lake Owasso.

Mac was outside with his teenage foster boys and Cheryl's teenage daughter, Sarah. They were having fun playing in the yard right next to the lake. Cheryl was watching all 5 teenagers throw softballs around with Mac when his house phone rang.

Because Mac was outside and his phone was inside, Cheryl answered it. She had done that before. A woman's voice was on the other end.

On July 15, Cheryl replayed that entire event again in her mind. In slow motion. Margaret asked for Mac and Cheryl told her that he was outside with the kids.

Margaret then asked, "So who are YOU?"

Cheryl said, "His fiancée. Who are you?"

Margaret replied with, "His FIANCEE?? ARE YOU KIDDING ME?! HE'S ENGAGED!!!?? WE HAVE TO TALK!!!!"

Cheryl took the call from Margaret in Mac's bedroom and locked the bedroom door while he was outside with the kids. The two women compared notes. It all matched up. The nights Cheryl was busy with her daughter at dance lessons, Mac was at Margaret's house. Having sex.

Mac was pounding on the door of his locked bedroom while the two women talked. Cheryl had the foresight to ask Margaret quickly for her phone number before Mac unlocked the door and raced in.

After Cheryl called off the wedding to Mac, the hardest part was picking up her wedding dress at the Wedding Shoppe on Grand Avenue in St. Paul. They would not take it back after alterations had been done and insisted she pick it up.

So she picked up a bride's wedding dress with no wedding to go to. Her heart was broken again.

It was an emotional experience she would never forget.

She thought about all of that ~ the entire experience with Mac and Margaret and the phone call on that other July afternoon so many years ago as she contemplated ending her own life. It was about the same time of year. Mid-July was what she remembered as the timeframe for that other traumatic phone call.

At least she didn't marry someone who would cheat on her. That was one thing she had done right.

After her experience with Mac, she called Bill every year on his birthday in October to wish him a Happy Birthday. He responded by calling her in March on her cell phone to wish her the same. This went on for over 20 years. The two of them talking twice a year. Always on their birthdays.

A few times over the years Cheryl went over to Bill's remodeled house in St. Louis Park. He had completely gutted a 1950's style house and created a magical new house. What Cheryl learned was that not only was he a talented Architect of million dollar homes, he was also very creative at redesigning modest homes.

On those rare occasions when she stopped over, Bill would make Cheryl dinner. He was an excellent cook. They both remembered what it was like to be 30-something.

On July 15th when Cheryl was contemplating ending her life she pondered all these things. Why didn't she give Bill more time? Then she might be living in a totally neat house in the suburbs where even the garbage can was clean!! She wouldn't be

TREA$URE YOUR LIFE | 15

considering ending her life over clutter, newspapers and not having a job.

She remembered how Michael entered into her life romantically after her breakup with Mac.

Michael was someone she had known for 12 years by working with him at the University of Minnesota. They were co-workers within the Information Technology Department. It was known as UCC (University Computer Center). They were also softball and tennis partners.

He recruited her to play on the U of M department team on her FIRST DAY of employment in that department. She barely had time to catch her breath, much less a softball.

He was the Coach.

On July 15, she remembered the day Michael walked into her office. She had just been shown her desk and was trying to settle in. The morning was already a blur.

The UCC department back then was full of energy and life. She remembered thinking there were about 150 people running around in circles and yet with a purpose. As if they were going places.

It was overwhelming with energy and activity. The University Computer Center. Not a boring place.

Quite different from the Engineering and Construction Department she had just spent the last 3 years of her life in at the University of Minnesota. That department had Engineers who were much older. The pace was slower.

He said to her quickly as if he was in a hurry, "You're the new one here today, right? Hi my name is Michael. Do you play softball?"

She said, "Well I've played it."

He replied, "That's good enough. We need more women. You're on the team."

Then he walked out. He had a clipboard in his hand that made him look official. He made a quick note and he was gone. That was it. It was that simple. No tryouts were necessary.

It all happened so fast. Their first meeting. Then it was over.

Over softball and tennis games they confided in each other through various relationships: Michael's divorce, Cheryl's break-up with Lee and Bill and Mac, Michael's breakup with his live-in girlfriend Annabel 6 years after his divorce.

In fact, they played softball on the same team for so long (over 25 years) that most of the team members married other members of the team. Cheryl would joke with people that their University Computer Center softball team "married itself".

Lillian and Dave, Janet and Jeff, Blake and Barb, Michael and Cheryl. Eight people on the same team married someone else who played on the team. What were the odds of that?

Cheryl remembered all this on the afternoon of July 15.

Her mind raced back to the moment she was attracted to Michael in a romantic way. After 12 years of knowing each other as friends and no longer working together at the U because Michael had gotten lucrative jobs at Apollo Computer Systems and other places, they discovered they were both out of relationships at the *same time*.

It was similar to the movie, '*When Harry Met Sally*' starring Meg Ryan and Billy Crystal. A movie they saw together at the Cooper Theatre in St. Louis Park when it first came out.

They had known each other through the worst of times. In fact, they always counted on each other through those worst of times.

Now after 20 years of marriage Cheryl had been trying to make a difference in the clutter of Michael's house. On July 15, she lost the battle.

Getting laid off from her Information Tech Manager job at the University of Minnesota several years before was the start of her depression. As the years wore on she became more and more depressed. Doing ANYTHING was an effort.

Michael tried to help her. He offered words of encouragement. He set up appointments with therapists and chiropractors. He even paid for it all. Cheryl had gone to her appointments but underneath it all she still felt worthless.

Cheryl's age was a factor in not getting job offers. She was 57. She was the same age as Oprah, John Travolta, Christie Brinkley, Ronnie Howard and Jerry Seinfeld. All who appeared to be doing well. All of them, including Cheryl, were born within the same 3 months of each other.

Compared to them, Cheryl felt completely unsuccessful and worthless.

Thinking about all of that was the reason why at 4:30 pm on a Friday afternoon in Minneapolis, only 3 hours after Michael left for the weekend, she was feeling MORE depressed and worthless than ever.

And she HADN'T EVEN BEEN DRINKING!!

I don't want to live anymore. My life is hopeless. I have no purpose.

She thought, "I can't handle the mess in this house. Nobody wants to hire me. We are going to lose the house if I don't get a job soon. I have to save us both. And now, I'm not even sexually attractive to my husband. No wonder he doesn't seem to want me like he used to."

He was more interested in Angie, one of the co-workers he met at an internet company after he left the University. A woman he had been having coffee and lunch with for the past 8 years. Angie was also married.

"It all makes sense to me now. Even Michael doesn't really want me anymore. He'd rather have Angie."

She was heart-broken once again. Rejection from her husband was the final straw. She was no longer sexually attractive to him ~ at least according to Sheridan.

Her mind was whirling. She had come to the end of her desire to live. She just wanted out.

* * *

So, how would I do it?

How would I take my own life?

Well, I could hang myself. But that has already been done in my family. Twice. It would not be original to do that. Besides, I think it would be painful to have your neck snap like that.

How about slashing my wrists? Nope, that's messy. I'd hate to leave a mess for people to clean up. Michael's sister tried doing herself in by slashing her throat and it was a disaster. Not only did she survive because Michael broke down the bathroom door and rescued her, but she lost so much blood in the process she became brain damaged. Michael's sister is now in a mental facility forced to take drugs every day just to maintain some sort of life. That's not how I want to be.

How about a gun? Nope. I don't have one. Never wanted one.

Hmmm... Jumping off a bridge? The Franklin Ave bridge over the Mississippi River is the closest one.

Nope. I'd hate for people to spend time looking for my body. I don't want to put anybody out. And have to deal with my body after being drowned.

I know what to do!!

I could take EVERYTHING in the medicine cabinet upstairs. I could show both Ralph and Dan how it's done. You just have to take plenty of stuff. Don't underestimate how much you'll need. Or you'll wind up in the psych ward at Abbott-Northwestern like they did.

That's also NOT a place I want to be on the INSIDE. If I'm going to do myself in, I want it to be successful! No psych ward for me. Although I do have to admit that both Ralph and Dan are doing fine. They've both recovered. It's being locked up that freaks me out.

Right now this minute I need to have SOMETHING done to success, in order to feel successful! Taking my own life will be it!

OK. Think fast! Don't change your mind this time. There were too many other times you changed your mind because you were scared. Assume if you take everything in the medicine cabinet upstairs you will be successful at doing yourself in.

And THEN WHAT??

As a Project Manager you have to think of all possible outcomes.

If we become dust after we die, then end of story.

That's it. No more. Done. Finished.

But what if we leave our bodies and become a Spirit?

And if as a Spirit, we are able to see and hear things that happen in the earthly world -- as if we are hovering as ghosts? People write about this sort of stuff, so you have to wonder.

Well, the first person to find me will be Sheridan. He promised to come back in 2 hours to check on me. He is a man of his word and will be here. I know him. He'll be on time. He always is.

He'll come right into the house. He even knows where the spare key is. If I'm dead, as a Spirit I'll have to watch him find me cold and unconscious. I'll be up here watching him shake me. (← She made a fist in her left hand and imagined him shaking her dead body).

He'll be saying frantically, "Cher! Cher! Please wake up!! Cher! What have you done?!!"

The police will be called.

It would be determined that I was dead. Sheridan would be devastated, wondering if what he said about the chaos and me not being sexually attractive to Michael pushed me over the edge.

As for Michael, nobody would know how to get ahold of him. I'm the only one who knows where he is. And I'm not even sure where that is. Some cabin up north? Did he take his cell phone with him? I don't remember.

Michael would have to wait until Sunday to find out his wife was dead.

Hmmmm….

I can just hear him tell his friends later that I seemed fine as he left for the weekend. The two guys who picked him up were witnesses. Both guys talked to me in the kitchen before they left. I was not depressed at all. I was looking forward to having the house to myself so that I could clean it. I even told them that.

The kitchen was a disaster. I had no problem with them seeing it as a mess. I knew I'd clean it up after they were gone.

Once Michael got the details about what Sheridan said to me would he kill Sheridan?

Maybe.

Then there'd be another death.

What about Sarah? My only child. The love of my life. She has kept me going all these years.

Sarah will be mad. I just know it.

She would hate me for taking my own life just as I was becoming useful to her again. By helping her do lawn work at her house, I was making a difference. By taking her dog for walks I was making a difference. I love my Grand Dog Riley. A beautiful and big Yellow Lab. I love him almost as much as Sarah does.

I remember how mad I was at Mom when she died. I tried to get her to stop smoking and drinking vodka but she just wouldn't. Who would have thought she'd have a heart attack at such a young age. 43??? How was that possible? I was only 22 years old. I was crushed.

I thought I'd *never* get over it. I remember having a hard time breathing when Dad told me she was gone. Wow. After only 24 hours in intensive care. While they were on vacation from Illinois to California to Oregon with my little brother, Terry who was 13 years old when she died.

Did that really happen? None of us could get there in time to say goodbye.

I know now that it was the beginning of the end of my first marriage. My husband John kept telling me to "Get over it."

Get over your mother dying??? How does one do that? She was my dear friend. We talked all the time. As much as we could afford to, anyway. We had to pay for long distance calls back then. She absolutely adored Sarah. Her first and only Grand Child.

Oh well. At least she got to be a Grandmother at the young age of 42. One year as a Grandmother. Better than nothing.

I should have tried harder to get her to stop smoking.

I got over it. You can't get somebody to stop smoking if they really don't want to. Just like with Cyndee. The Maid of Honor in my 2nd marriage. My marriage to Michael. I had to watch her die in the hospital a couple of years after Michael and I got married because she smoked too much.

That was tough. I used to cry to get Cyndee to stop smoking when we went out as single women because I told her my mother died from smoking. But Cyndee never stopped. My tears had no effect on her.

My good friend Cyndee was barely 40 years old. Way too young to die.

Back to Mom.

I realized that I would have rather had MY mother for 22 years of my life than some OTHER people's mothers. It was the Woman Within organization which helped me see that. My mother loved life and people. She used cigarettes and vodka to cope with her own issues but never yelled at anybody.

So, Sarah would be upset with me if I took my own life. In time she would probably get over it through therapy. I did.

What about Dad? With another suicide in the family this could really affect him. Who knows how well his heart would hold up? Maybe he'd have a heart attack?

Then there'd be another death…

My brothers, Jerry and Terry would go on without their sister. I've been sort of a pain to them lately so this could be a blessing. They seem irritated with me these last few years. They don't call very much anymore. They're busy with their own lives. They think I'm just too depressed.

I have no sisters.

The closest thing I had to sisters were my Woman Within friends. Oh yeah – that's right. I *had*. They *were*. They've rejected me now too. My entire E-circle of Woman Within friends won't miss me at all.

E-circle stood for Empowerment Circle. They abandoned me and forced me out of their group at a time when I needed them the most. Six weeks after Dee, died. My wonderful 2nd mother. She was awesome!

I begged the E-circle group NOT to kick me out. They all knew my depression started after I got laid off from the University of Minnesota.

They insisted that I get a year of therapy before coming back to the group.

How am I going to pay for therapy? I don't have a job!

"That's not for us to decide," they said.

Who suddenly took over in the group and demanded that I get a year of therapy in order to stop my depression? And then come up with the idea that I needed to have signed therapist's papers to prove I was **worthy** of coming back to the E-circle after an entire year! Where did that come from?

What women Bully took over and coerced the rest of the group to kick me out?

The Woman Within organization was supposed to be a support group. It was **unthinkable** that an E-circle would do that to a member.

Especially under those conditions: the recent death of a family member. My 2nd Mom.

I think I know who was behind it.

Was I hurting anybody in the group? Nope. Was I in danger of hurting anybody in society? Nope. I was simply depressed.

I remember not staying that night to take the beads from the necklace as the leader wanted me to. I remember saying, "If you are going to cut me out of the E-circle tonight, you're just going to have to deal with the beads yourself. I'm not taking them."

It had a negative effect on my ability to cope with Dee's death. I couldn't even talk about being rejected from the E-circle group with Michael. It was too painful.

Why did those women do that?

I must be worthless.

Oh yeah. Then there's Ann. She wouldn't miss me at all if I killed myself. She was my best friend from the University.

Again, she *was*. We used to talk on the phone every day even though we no longer worked together. Outside of the Woman Within group she was like a sister to me. We even adopted each other as sisters. Neither one of us had any real sisters. We only had brothers.

It's been a few months since Ann told me our friendship had to be 'put on hold.' Put on hold?? What in the world does that mean? She said something about getting too emotionally involved in my problems and needing a break. A break? From your Best Friend's problems!??

I shouldn't have been so depressed. If I hadn't been so depressed Ann would never have given up our friendship. I lost her. It's all my fault.

The last message I got from Ann was when I raced down the stairs to answer my cell phone only to hear a voice mail that said, "Sorry Cheryl that I missed you. I'm really busy these days. I'll call you when I can."

In other words, "Don't call me. I'll call you."

The call from Ann never came.

An additional slap in the face came after I realized Ann had Un-Friended me on Facebook. Wow. The Ultimate Humiliation.

I must be worthless. Ann doesn't call me anymore and she used to call every day.

Now I only have one girlfriend left in the Minneapolis area that I talk to on a regular basis. I remember when Fran and I were walked out the door on the same day from the University. They gave us no chance to say goodbye to anybody.

Just like when my mother died. No chance to say goodbye.

It was a cold day in March, several years ago. Two days after I turned 49 years old. The reason they gave us was 'Budget Cuts'. But in my case, the layoff turned out to be because I was a

TREA$URE YOUR LIFE | 27

whistleblower to Tari's $1,000,000 excessive spending of taxpayer's money.

Tari became my boss through what I call a 'Freak Reorg': A reorganization where nothing makes sense. She had only been my boss for about 6 months when she laid me off.

Tari was relatively new to the University and not familiar with the internal workings or networks of people. Neither was Rod. Her boss. They were both from outside the U.

I remember the contracts Tari and Rod arranged for $200,000 each with separate companies to bring in consultants for a major PeopleSoft upgrade project. Many of the consultants they brought in were their friends. We didn't need that many consultants for the PeopleSoft upgrade. A few would have been fine. Not several.

Their friends were not all that effective as consultants. They were difficult to understand and not very personable. It was obvious the consultants were part of their elite clique.

Tari told us on the management team that by having multiple contracts with separate vendors at $200,000 each they could stay under the Regent's radar. The Regents of the University of Minnesota had to approve all projects over $250,000.

I remember the look of glee in her eyes when Tari said that to us in a meeting. Like they were getting away with something. She and Rod were behind it.

I figured out that separate contracts for the same project – a PeopleSoft upgrade – totaled over $1,000,000. It was incomprehensible to a lot of people within the U that 'they' could get away with this without the Regent's approval! Those of us on the management team were talking about it.

Were Tari and Rod *above* the approval process??

The two of them were abusing their management privileges in many other ways by traveling all over the country to attend PeopleSoft conferences. They were acting like Enron upper management with their luxurious spending habits. Staying in expensive hotels. Eating out every night. Entertaining others.

All on taxpayer's money.

I remember when I went to Stanley ~ the CIO ~ on my own to express my concerns over their spending habits. It was my taxpayer's money, too, that they were wasting!!

I had known Stanley over 20 years. He was one of *us*. He would understand, I figured. He was so high up the ladder by that time that he probably wasn't even aware of what those under him were doing.

Stanley listened to my concerns but at the end of our conversation in his private office within Morrill Hall he appeared to be uncomfortable.

I remember him telling me nervously that he would talk to Tari that weekend. He was flying to New Orleans over the weekend with her to attend a PeopleSoft conference.

My heart sank as he told me this.

He also told me that staying under the Regent's radar with multiple contracts was something that happened at the University of Minnesota often. Other departments did it, too.

My heart sank further.

My first thought was that I didn't even know there *was* another PeopleSoft conference the next week! It wasn't announced to us.

How could those of us on the management team not know there was a PeopleSoft conference in New Orleans? Were Stanley and Tari the only ones going? Nobody from my area was going, that was for sure. PeopleSoft conferences were primarily for technical programmers, web designers and managers. Neither Tari nor Stanley were technical PeopleSoft managers!!

The CIO was attending a PeopleSoft conference??!

Going from Minnesota in the cold Winter to warm New Orleans for a week would have been a treat.

My second thought was that he knew and approved of what Tari and Rod were doing. I wasn't telling him anything new.

"I'm dead," I remember thinking. Stanley was one of *them*.

As a reward for going to the CIO, I wound up on the layoff list a week later ... after 24 years of dedicated service with outstanding reviews. Who would have thought? My co-workers were totally shocked!

I remember the day I went to Stanley with my concerns. It was a cold gray January day in Minnesota. The week of Martin Luther King's birthday. It was cold outside with a lot of white snow everywhere.

After the dust had settled on my layoff and I was gone from the U, my internal sources told me that I was on the official layoff list by the last week in January. One week after I talked to Stanley. Right after he came back from a PeopleSoft conference in New Orleans with Tari. And well BEFORE there was any hint of a Budget Crisis within the University of Minnesota.

My actual layoff date was March 5. The significance of this was that during the month of February there were articles in the Minneapolis Star and Tribune paper identifying unexpected state budget cuts for the University that were going into effect on March 1st.

I asked Tari in a manager's meeting at the end of February (not knowing anything about being on the layoff list) if there were going to be any layoffs during the Budget Crisis of that March.

She said to me somewhat nervously during the meeting, "No, Cheryl, there will be no layoffs. I can assure you. None. Absolutely none."

And 5 days later on Wednesday, I got laid off.

Why did I get laid off after I told my entire PeopleSoft team in a meeting right afterwards that Tari assured us there would be *no layoffs* during the Budget Crisis??

It was obvious she was lying to me. I had been on the layoff list since the last week in January after talking to Stanley. Tari was my 'boss' and had been so for approximately 6 months. It was March. She had to have known.

She had flown to New Orleans with Stanley to attend a PeopleSoft conference in late January. It doesn't take an Einstein to figure that one out.

The sudden layoff was traumatic for me. I never really recovered. I felt totally betrayed by my good 'friend' Stanley. I had always been rewarded for doing the right thing and now I was being punished for doing what I thought was the right thing: Reporting outlandish spending habits to the CIO.

The Wednesday I got laid off was a U of M bowling night. I was scheduled to bowl. I showed up for bowling totally in shock and saw my co-workers looking at me. People started crying when they saw me, and then I did too. I remember being in a fog as those around me were in tears trying to understand what had happened.

My bowling team started hugging me. I had been walked out the door like a criminal without getting a chance to say goodbye to my PeopleSoft team. That had never happened before in our OIT department.

I don't want to work for an organization that is not going to listen to their employees.

I don't want to live anymore. It's not worth it. I want out of this life.

Fran would be really upset if I was dead.

So would Anastasia even though we don't talk very much anymore. Anastasia is a piano player like me who works in the information technology world. She is incredibly intelligent. We can relate to each other because of the piano connection.

She is so busy now I hardly ever see her. She is traveling all over the world doing presentations. She goes regularly to Australia and New Zealand for conferences where she presents papers on Business Process Redesign (BPR). I still feel close to her because we connected so quickly. But we don't talk much anymore and rarely see each other.

It would be hard as a Spirit to watch both Fran and Anastasia go through the pain of having to deal with my death. I introduced them to each other. They stay in touch so they would probably talk about my suicide and wonder if there was anything they could have done.

Fran would also talk to Ann (my former 'sister') from the University because the 3 of us worked very closely together as managers. We all ran 5K races together.

In fact, Fran and Ann and Anastasia now all know each other. The 4 of us had lunch together at Ann's house. On a beautiful summer day a few years ago. I remember the wind blowing gently through the screens of Ann's porch. The sun was shining. It was a perfect Minnesota day.

It seems so long ago. The only time the 4 of us ever had lunch together. So many things have changed since then.

Her thoughts continued to race as she contemplated ending her life.

And then there's Sally. My high school friend. Sally who was the Maid of Honor in my 1st wedding when I married John, my high school sweetheart. I was Sally's Maid of Honor in her wedding 9 months later when she married Greg.

Greg. My next door Neighbor. The Cute Guy I grew up with next door who married my Best Friend Sally. And is *still* married to him.

Ah yes, I remember the weekend of their wedding when John and I drove down from the Upper Peninsula of Michigan to be in the wedding. John was an usher. I was the Maid of Honor.

It was the weekend I got pregnant with Sarah.

TREA$URE YOUR LIFE

The one weekend in my marriage that I threw the birth control out the window because I figured it wouldn't matter.

I was married after all. I was 20 years old and madly in love with my Husband. So WHAT if I got pregnant? I just wasn't quite ready, that was all. I felt a bit young. And somewhat reckless.

John and I had a wild weekend at Sally and Greg's wedding partying constantly. We loved being back home again in New Brighton (a suburb of Minneapolis and St. Paul) with our high school friends.

Who would have thought 9 months later that Sarah would come into this world? It's amazing how friends can influence your life in a big way.

How has Sally managed to keep our connection going these many years since high school? We've never even lived in the same state since graduation from Irondale!! She's been in Connecticut, Iowa and California. I've mostly been here in Minnesota. But also in Illinois and Michigan.

It's because of *her* that we even talk. Not me. She's the one who's always reaching out to me. Calling me and sending cards. I hardly do anything.

She would be upset if I did myself in. Especially after all her efforts to remain in touch these many years. So would Greg. My Neighbor. I still call him that.

A few people around me would probably be feeling some sense of loss.

A funeral would happen.

As a Spirit, I'd have to watch people go through the funeral experience, while hearing them say in hushed breaths, "She killed herself. Isn't it tragic? She had so much going for her."

That's what people usually say at suicide funerals. So much going for her?? I felt totally worthless. What did I have going for me? Not much. That's for sure.

How would I handle all the guilt as a Spirit?

I wonder how everyone's lives would go on without me.

Sheridan would find another workout partner at Bally's. Michael would probably get married again. Sally and Fran and Anastasia would find other close friends but would be upset with me for taking my life.

Sarah my only child would go through therapy but would probably get over her mother dying, even if it was because of suicide.

And Dad, if he didn't have a heart attack, would deal with it. He always does.

But as a Spirit, I'd have to live with the pain of choosing to give up my own life forever.

* * *

As Cheryl pondered that thought for many minutes, she imagined the next steps of her Life trying to beg God for another chance.

Please God, give me my life back. I didn't mean it. I changed my mind. I didn't mean to hurt all these people. I just didn't want to live anymore in the mess and the clutter.

And without a Job or a Purpose. I don't want to feel useless anymore. It doesn't pay to do the right thing. You just get punished. If you are at all successful at your job some insecure woman gets jealous and takes it all away from you.

But God would probably say,

> "Sorry, Cheryl, this is not a movie. It's not *'It's A Wonderful Life'* ~ with Jimmy Stewart. You made the decision. You had a choice. You decided to take your own life. You don't get another chance.
>
> Even I ~ as God with my Infinite Powers cannot give you your life back. Now you have to live with this for the rest of your Spiritual Life."

That could be a long time.

How long is one's spiritual life, anyway?

Chapter 2 ~ The Decision

Cheryl pondered ending her own life for some time. In her mind it was an Eternity. In Reality it was about 30 minutes. Her mind was racing through all the events of her life that led her to this point. Through the years. From Past to Present. And back again.

The Project Manager in her mind kept asking the phrase:

> '*... And THEN what??*'

What would it be like to experience the guilt of hurting people around her – as a Spirit?

And to live with this guilt forever... How long would that be????

Time stopped for her ~ she found herself going back and forth between two worlds. Here and Eternity. Now and the Afterlife. Life and Death.

She didn't want to live in *either* place. She felt worthless in the Current Life but figured she might hate herself in the Other Life.

She wished someone would come through the door with a gun and put her out of her misery. But nobody did. Not on a stormy rainy Friday afternoon in July.

I hate myself. I hate this life. I am worthless and nobody wants to hire me. Almost all my friends are gone. They don't want me, either. Neither does my family.

She said to herself, "I want Time to stop while I figure this out. And yet, I want to make a decision and move forward. Any type of decision. Just so that I make one. This indecision is sheer torture!!"

As she thought back to the Present Moment she moved from her living room where she had been pondering ending her life to the mess in the sun porch. It was overwhelming.

I hate living with all this clutter! I hate not having a job! I hate not having a Purpose! I hate feeling useless!!

She realized it wasn't just the mess ~ it was also the lack of a job. Due to the economy, jobs were scarce. What could she do about it now? She had taken some Project Manager jobs since she had gotten laid off from the University of Minnesota but she always lost interest as soon as she started feeling emotionally connected to a job.

She didn't want to go through the devastation of having something taken away from her that she loved, so she *never* loved a job again after losing her job at the U. She never let herself get attached emotionally to any organization or job.

The layoff from the University also devastated her because she thought she was doing the right thing. She had reported outlandish spending practices to the CIO ~ only to be thrown away so quickly.

She trusted Stanley. What a mistake that was.

On July 15, she remembered the humiliation of going through countless interviews since her layoff and having to explain why after 24 years of service at the University did she get laid off for Budget Cuts? She never told people the real story in interviews. All her job counseling and workshops had people who suggested she keep emotions in check and talk positively about former bosses.

Even after taking new jobs it was demoralizing for her to start at the bottom of the ladder and have to prove herself. She had proven herself to be successful at getting many projects done over her 24 years of service.

Why did she have to start at the bottom again?

Not only that, she found herself very indecisive because of the layoff having trouble making any kind of decisions on the job. Or deciding which job to take! It was making her crazy second-guessing herself.

She didn't trust her own decisions anymore. About anything. Even simple things like ordering menu items in a restaurant.

ALL decisions were becoming difficult. She read somewhere that it was a sign of severe depression when decisions were impossible to make. It used to be easy for her to make decisions. Now *any* decision paralyzed her.

Even when she finally made a decision on anything she usually changed her mind. It drove her family nuts. Especially her Dad and her two brothers.

She found herself bored with other jobs. She grew weary and tired in meetings. It was all pointless because no matter how successful she was at her job it was going to be taken away from her. Nothing mattered to her anymore.

You only got punished for working hard. Some Woman was going to get jealous and take it all away from you.

Like a Bully.

She shouldn't have gone to Stanley – the CIO – with her concerns. That was a mistake.

Here she was, 8 years later on a Friday afternoon in July feeling the effects of the layoff. She and Michael were financially strapped. He kept telling her she needed to get a Job or they were going to lose the house. His precious house. His Castle. Foreclosure could be their future.

Homelessness was something she worried about constantly.

Her mind kept racing round and round in circles.

It was a mistake to trust Stanley. Someone she thought was her Friend. He really wasn't. He was one of *them*. How could she have been so Stupid as to trust him???

As the thunderstorms continued outside it was as dark at 4:30 pm in the afternoon as it was at night. It had been raining all afternoon. It was storming even as Michael left earlier that day. She remembered him getting soaked by the rain as he got into the car with the other guys.

Time stopped for her while she analyzed the situation…

* * *

After several minutes of emotional turmoil, she realized that maybe ending one's life might NOT be such a smart thing to do. Hating herself in the After Life and imagining begging God for a 2nd chance was what finally caused her to pause for a moment.

She realized that once she crossed over the edge from this Life to the next and was successful at it, there was NO going back. And if it was by *her* choice, not a random act of violence she would ultimately feel guilty over it.

God was *not* going to give her a 2nd chance. She would be stuck on the *other* side.

Forever.

No possibility of going back. Especially if she changed her mind. Which she often did these days. On just about anything.

What to do?

Cheryl suddenly saw a bolt of lightening while looking out the windows and at the same time heard a CLAP! of thunder. She let out a scream because it startled her ~ and then realized that maybe she could do ONE thing on the sun porch.

That's what Sheridan suggested.

"Just do ONE thing. ANYTHING."

Those were his last words to her.

She looked around. She was standing at the door leading to the sun porch. She saw papers, bags, boxes, golf clubs, clothes, magazines, pictures and piles of mail. There was so much clutter and chaos that she could not walk from the entrance of the sun porch to the couch without crawling over bags or papers or boxes or clothes.

"God, what should I do?"

She felt totally overwhelmed and worthless, once again unable to decide anything.

And then she saw them.

The screens for all the porch windows were stacked up near the door. There were 11 screens in all – each one 3 feet wide by 4 feet. She had taken the screens off the windows last year because she planned to wash the windows. Today it was raining and it would NOT be a good day to wash windows.

She wondered how a year could have gone by without moving the screens at all. The screens had been stacked there in the sun porch for an entire *year*. How was that possible??

Putting the screens back up *without* washing the windows didn't make sense. She'd just have to take them off again later to wash the windows.

But putting the screens up did have an advantage in that it would get them out of the way. She remembered the last words Sheridan spoke to her about doing something – it really didn't matter what. ANYTHING!!

"Just DO something." She heard his words to her again.

"I guess I could put *one* of these screens back up on the window. It's easy to do that."

She went over to the stack of screens and put one up in about 10 seconds. Then she did another. And another. Before she knew it she had all 11 screens back up on the windows. This had the unexpected side benefit of creating space of 3 feet by 4 feet by 1 foot in the sun porch.

A Baby Step towards progress.

Plus it gave her a sense of accomplishment.

Finally!!!

"I DID something! Now Sheridan will be able to see that I made progress."

She stopped and looked at her watch. She still had 1 hour and 30 minutes before he was set to come back and check on her.

Hmmmmm….

She took another minute to roll open the windows. With the screens up it meant flies and other insects could be kept out. The windows had been closed all summer giving the sun porch a stuffy closed up smell. After opening the windows she smelled the rain from outside.

The air was cool coming through the windows even though it was mid-July. The cool air was a relief from the heat. The air even SMELLED good with the fresh rain smell from the outside.

With new eyes she noticed the wooden sill of the first window. It was filthy. It had accumulated black dirt and dust blowing in over the last couple of years. Cheryl couldn't remember the last time she cleaned it.

"I guess I could get some Lemon Pledge from under the sink and clean it. Just this *one window sill*. That's it. Then I'll be done."

"I'll be able to show Sheridan that I did More than One Thing."

TREA$URE YOUR LIFE

She went to the kitchen and got the Pledge along with some paper towels. In 10 seconds she had the dirty black window sill cleaned. It was a beautiful mahogany brown again!!

She looked at the next one. Before she knew it she cleaned that one too. And the next one. And the next one. In 10 minutes, all 11 window sills were cleaned. They all went from black to brown.

Beautiful wood underneath it all.

She stood back to admire her work. And she felt good.

She looked at her watch again. She still had 1 hour and 20 minutes before Sheridan was going to come bounding through the door. Standing on the sun porch with Pledge in her hand in the middle of thunder and lightning and rain outside, she noticed how dirty the wooden frame had gotten on the French doors from Michael's living room leading to the sun porch. So she cleaned the wood frame on that, too.

She hadn't cleaned the French doors in all her 20 years of marriage to Michael.

Spraying Pledge all over the French door frame had the side effect of getting the wax spray on the glass windows of the French doors, so she decided to get some Windex for the glass. A few minutes later, she finished that job.

She cleaned all the window panes on the French doors leading to the sun porch.

She stood back to admire her work.

She had NEVER cleaned the French doors before!! Stepping into Michael's living room and looking through the newly cleaned

French door windows caused her to pause and see the mess in the sun porch as if for the first time.

The doors were sparkling but the sun porch was still a mess.

She glanced at her watch. Now she only had 1 hour and 10 minutes before Sheridan came back. She saw her round glass wicker table in the sun porch. The table was piled high with mail and other papers. She looked at the bottle of Windex in her hand and wished she could clean the glass table top ~ but that would mean she'd have to deal with the clutter on the table.

Fueled by Energy from her recent accomplishments she tackled the clutter on the table. One piece at a time.

Baby Steps.

It turned out to be mostly junk mail. All of it was fairly easily discarded into the recycle pile. The few important papers were put into a small pile for filing later.

And to think it's been like this for 6 months!! What was I thinking? None of this is really needed.

She felt an even greater sense of accomplishment when she was able to spray the entire glass table with Windex. She stopped to look at her watch. Wow! She still had 1 hour before Sheridan came back! It had only taken her 10 minutes to clean off the entire glass table.

She put the Windex down, grabbed the Pledge and proceeded to clean the wicker on all the oversized chairs in the sun porch. The chairs were thick with dust. She had not cleaned them in her 20 years of marriage.

The lemony smell of Pledge combined with the fresh smell of rain through the open windows had turned her into a cleaning tornado.

She went from the wicker chairs to tackling other bags of papers and clothes. The golf clubs went downstairs. Clothes went to the laundry basket. More junk mail in bags went to the recycling pile. Art objects from her dad's condo in Florida were distributed in other places throughout the house. Valuable papers went into a special pile to be filed later.

Plastic bottles with some juice or water left in them went to the recycle bin. Garbage went to the wastebasket in the kitchen, which became full.

As she raced against Time… she noticed how much energy she had. Decisions were easy to make. With each decision the next one became easier. No more Procrastination. Now it was a race with herself to see how much she could get done before Sheridan came back.

After all, she was Alive! She didn't have to beg for her life back from God.

Thank God! She felt relieved.

At promptly 6:30 pm her cell phone rang. She saw it was Sheridan. Cheryl was getting ready to vacuum the rose colored carpeting in the sun porch. It was a carpet she hadn't seen in over a year. It had been covered with papers, clothes and other clutter. Now it was completely clean from all the stuff!! It just needed vacuuming.

He was calling to say he'd be there in 5 minutes. He was just leaving Bally's after swimming with Colleen. One thing about Sheridan was that if he said he'd be there, he really was.

And on time, too.

She told him over the phone, "OK. Should I stop watching TV now?"

Sheridan paused for a few seconds and then said, "Yes."

Cheryl wondered what prompted her to say that. She was NOT watching TV. She was busy cleaning the sun porch. The TV had been off the whole time. Her banter with Sheridan was unpredictable. She had known him 10 years. They teased each other more than they teased anybody else.

She was still vacuuming the rose colored carpeting when Sheridan came bounding into her house as advertised. He went right through both living rooms to the sun porch door and stopped in total amazement.

"WHAT THE ----?!!!!" He exclaimed as his eyes got wide in astonishment.

"Well", said Cheryl, "Can you tell that I've done anything?"

In typical Sheridan fashion, he suddenly became very cool and looked around. "You know I'm an Inspector…"

"Uh-huh," she replied.

He said this often -- that he was an Inspector. He used to work for Medtronic – the heart pacemaker company headquartered in Minneapolis. He had to inspect all kinds of heart pacemakers at close range.

"And as an Inspector I notice things."

TREA$URE YOUR LIFE | 47

"Uh-huh"… So what have you noticed?"

"Hmmm…" He looked around the totally cleaned sun porch.

He said very calmly, "You put the screens up."

"Yup", she replied. "You noticed."

He looked around some more. "You cleaned the window sills."

Now that's spooky, she thought. It was the 2nd thing she had done. But he was after all, an Inspector.

"So, did you notice anything else?" She asked.

"Well", he said. "Wasn't there something on this table?"

He pointed to the glass table on the sun porch. It had been piled high with 12 inches of papers before he left for swimming and now the table was completely cleaned. Even Windexed.

They both laughed hysterically.

Cheryl thought, "That was the 3rd thing I cleaned on the sun porch. What was up with that??!! How in the world did he know?"

"You DID notice! Yes, there were lots of things on that table. Most of it junk mail. You ARE an Inspector, after all."

He looked at her incredulously and said, "What the heck happened here???"

"Well, Sher, I got to thinking about the mess and decided I was either going to kill myself over the clutter or clean it up. It was that simple."

"You were going to WHAT?!!!"

"Yup, you heard me. I was going to do myself in. But I didn't think I'd get another chance after that. My life isn't a movie, you know. It's NOT *'A Wonderful Life.'* God probably wouldn't give me another chance."

As Sheridan tried to comprehend what she was saying and realized she was not kidding, he became very distraught. He knew from working out with her every morning over the past 3 years that she had become very depressed. She always talked about wanting to go back in Time and do things differently.

Over and over again.

"Cher, I need to explain that comment I said to you that made you cry."

"Oh, what was that, Sher?" She asked innocently.

Knowing full well what it was.

He said, "It was the comment about this place being a 'cock block'. I had no right to say that. I don't know how Michael feels about your sex life and you've never indicated you had any problems with that. I got to thinking while I was swimming… you know I really have a lot of time to do that by swimming laps for an hour and I realized my comment was really directed at Katherine. Not *you*. It's HER chaos and hoarding that really turns ME off."

Katherine was Sheridan's girlfriend. She was a classic hoarder. Sheridan was living with her and trying to make a difference. He was losing the battle. No matter what he did to organize her place and make it livable she continued to bring more stuff in. Almost on a daily basis.

TREA$URE YOUR LIFE | 49

The clutter in Katherine's house had finally turned Sheridan off to having any kind of sex with her. The mess was too chaotic.

As Katherine left every morning for her job as a Nurse's aide in a local hospital, Sheridan tried to clean and organize her duplex. He was living frugally from his investments and savings.

He seemed to be managing but lately had begun to complain about her mess. He could never get above it. He was not working at a job and yet was managing to survive by his investments and cheap lifestyle.

The house Sheridan owned was on the same block as Katherine's rented duplex. His house was completely paid for. He had no monthly mortgage. He had only taxes, electric, lights and heat to pay.

He had renters Ron and Karen, living in his house. He still had access to his upstairs bedroom. But he was hardly ever there. He spent so much time trying to organize Katherine's mess that it took him out of the work he needed to do on his own house.

His house was located near the University of Minnesota. Just like Cheryl and Michael's house. Cheryl was on one side of the major train tracks going through Dinkytown and he was on the other. They often heard the same train whistle when they talked on the phone.

The reason Katherine didn't live in Sheridan's house was because of her excessive amount of stuff. Katherine refused to have a sale to get rid of anything.

She couldn't give up her multiple blenders, crock pots, purses, cooking bowls, bathroom items, brushes, sunglasses, coats and clothes and shoes she never wore. All still in their original cheap packaging with price tags. From Goodwill-type thrift stores. For lower income people.

None of it was being used. Katherine kept bringing in more stuff. Almost every day. In plain white plastic bags. Sometimes she brought stuff home in large purse-type bags that still had price tags on the purses, and the purses were not in other plastic bags.

Cheryl remembered on July 15 another morning when Sheridan drove Katherine's car to pick up Cheryl for their 5 am Bally's workout and he showed Cheryl the trunk of Katherine's car. It was full of large cloth bags with price tags on them stuffed with cheap discount items. From thrift stores.

Cheryl remembered him saying to her that morning, "Look at all this crap!! The back seat is full to the top with stuff that she doesn't need either! It just drives me *crazy*!"

Her first floor of the duplex was filled with so much stuff it was hard to navigate through rooms. There was no place to sit. The furniture was buried under mountains of clothes and clutter. The basement was full to the top, too. The kitchen table was so full of stuff that there was no place to sit at the table.

Cheryl remembered seeing all this when she helped Sheridan move in to Katherine's duplex down the street. He had hardly any room for his few clothes.

Katherine was very similar to Michael in Cheryl's life.

In addition to Katherine's mess, the thorn in Sheridan's side was his *own* mess. His garage. He couldn't get a handle on organizing it. He had gotten into the habit of bringing home items discarded on the sidewalk by other people's houses that he didn't need on a regular basis.

Just like Katherine.

Both Sheridan and Cheryl had degenerated into the messy lifestyle of their respective partners. They were living in arrangements like Oscar and Felix from the TV show ~ The Odd Couple. Even though Sheridan and Cheryl in their hearts were Neatniks, they had given up trying to organize their living areas.

Before he went swimming, as Sheridan looked around Cheryl's house and saw the clutter everywhere he lost his temper because he realized that he was totally surrounded by Chaos.

Everywhere in his life!! Even in Cheryl's house. The house they had cleaned only 2 years before!

He told her that the idea of the chaos and clutter completely turned HIM off to sex with Katherine. Or anybody else for that matter. It was too much. He figured it was the same for any guy looking at chaos and clutter. That's why he said what he did before he went swimming.

After swimming, when Sheridan saw Cheryl's newly cleaned sun porch he became energized. As Cheryl continued vacuuming the rose colored carpet she hadn't seen in over a year, Sheridan noticed the Nordic track in the corner of the sun porch. Before she realized it, Sheridan had taken apart the entire corner. It was an area she wasn't going to touch.

The corner contained Michael's stuff.

"What are you doing??!!!" She exclaimed!

"Just organizing stuff," he replied.

"But that's Michael's stuff!!! He'll have a fit!!"

"Too bad, I'm on a roll. Get out of my way." Sheridan continued to pull stuff out of the corner of the sun porch.

Cheryl figured it wasn't going to hurt for the corner to be organized, too. After all, she had done 90% of the work so far. Organizing stuff was Sheridan's thing. She decided not to stop him. As Sheridan took out the Nordic track and the other stuff crammed into the corner, one of the things he pulled out was pillows.

"Now's my chance to really make a difference!!!" She thought. She wanted to make a difference in the house while Michael was gone for the weekend. That meant to actually throw stuff away. Michael wasn't home to stop her.

Or pull stuff back out of the garbage.

Cheryl collected two armfuls of pillows that Sheridan pulled out of the sun porch corner.

They were pillows for furniture covered with years of dust. She had purchased them over time and then gradually stopped using them – because she bought other ones.

She knew that throwing her pillows out (the throw pillows ~ no pun intended) in their own garbage can would result in a future argument with Michael if he found them in their garbage can outside.

This happened often.

She could just hear Michael, "Why are you throwing these perfectly good pillows away?!!"

It would lead to an argument. Then frustration for both of them as Michael would pull stuff back *out* of the garbage. It was appropriate that Sheridan was cleaning out this corner giving her free reign to throw out the dusty pillows. Without Michael telling her *not* to throw them out.

They were *her* pillows after all. She bought them, she should have the right to throw them away if they were no longer needed.

With her arms full of pillows she headed out the back door. Down the stairs of the back yard and out to the gate. She opened the gate and then looked around the street surreptitiously before sneaking across to the Luxton Park neighborhood dumpster.

She wasn't about to throw the pillows in her *own* garbage can.

As Cheryl was crossing the street, an old woman was sitting on her front door step in Luxton Park watching her. The woman called out, "Hey M'aam. Are you tryin' da trow dose pillows away?"

Cheryl froze. Oh NO I've been caught! If not by Michael, then by this older woman. Cheryl couldn't seem to throw stuff away anymore – no matter how hard she tried. What was up with that??

"Lemme see dose pillows."

"Oh – you don't really want these pillows. They're really dirty."

"Lemme *see* 'em!" Said the older woman emphatically.

Reluctantly, Cheryl walked over to the doorstep of where the old woman was sitting. The woman quickly inspected the pillows and said they were of high quality. They just needed a washing.

Cheryl told her that if the pillows didn't survive the washer, the woman could throw them away in the neighborhood dumpster. She found out the woman's name was Martha.

A few days later she ran into Martha again by the street. Cheryl asked Martha how the pillows came out. "Oh I looove dose pillows! I had to run 'em trew da washer. TWICE!! But dey look beeaautiful!! I have 'em on ma bed upstairs and ma couch downstairs."

Who would have thought? At least they didn't wind up in the neighborhood dumpster.

Back to the sun porch story.

With Sheridan pulling out everything in the corner and Cheryl finishing up putting things away, the sun porch was truly coming alive. If a porch could be thought of as coming alive this one was it.

The rain stopped and the sun was setting as they finished the final cleaning together. They worked well as a team. Just like they worked together after the fire 2 years before while Michael was in Texas.

It was around 8:30 pm on Friday, July 15th. The sun porch looked beautiful. It was lit up as the evening sun's rays came through the large windows and across the room. Truly a magical place.

TREA$URE YOUR LIFE

They both stopped to enjoy the sunset. The rays coming across the backyard into the newly cleaned sun porch were absolutely breathtaking.

Cheryl looked at Sheridan and said, "Are you hungry?"

He replied, "Now that you mention it… I am."

Cheryl grabbed some frozen steaks out of the freezer and grilled them outside. They enjoyed a candlelight steak dinner with Chardonnay on the newly cleaned wicker table and lost track of time.

They could see the full moon rising in the sky from the sun porch when they finally realized what time it was. It was 3 am. They had been having so much fun talking and enjoying their cleaning efforts that time slipped away.

The Time that stopped for Cheryl earlier in the day was now flying past her. She was no longer having problems making decisions. Cleaning the sun porch gave her hope.

She was successful again at something.

Cheryl asked Sheridan if Katherine would wonder where he was at 3 am. "Nope, she thinks I'm with Colleen tonight, watching a movie", he told her.

Sheridan had a platonic relationship with his swimming partner Colleen and often spent the night on Colleen's couch in her townhouse after watching a movie Friday night. Katherine was used that that routine.

He was too tired to drive home. He didn't want to wake Katherine up at 3 am or go to his own house and wake his renters up at that hour by going upstairs to his bedroom.

The night ended wonderfully with Sheridan sleeping on Cheryl's couch in the sun porch.

They both fell asleep exhausted.

Chapter 3 ~ The Dragonfly

Cheryl woke up around 6 am Saturday morning remembering the story she told Sheridan the previous night while they were having their sunset dinner –

> "Michael told me the sun porch was one of the reasons he bought this house with his first wife, Carol. The morning sun shines from the East and the evening sun comes from the West.
>
> When I married Michael and moved in after his divorce and break-up with his girlfriend, the sun porch was full to the ceiling with boxes of newspapers. It was a disaster. I had to put my foot down and force him to take boxes out of here in order for my wicker dining room set to fit in.
>
> He had only half of the newspapers gone after the first month.
>
> I still remember one of the first meals we had in this sun porch. Dad came up from Chicago for some meetings here in Minneapolis during our 2nd month of marriage. I offered to cook him dinner. It was Michael, Sarah, Dad and me eating on my wicker table set. A mountain of newspapers still existed in the sun porch. The couch was completely buried beneath newspapers.
>
> Dad looked up at the wall of newspaper boxes, looked at me quizzically and wondered what the newspapers were doing in there. Nothing in my dad's house was out of place. He

and his wife, Dee, were Neatniks. In his opinion I was living in a *total* mess.

I told him that the sun porch used to be FULL of newspapers and this was great progress. Half the newspapers were gone! At least I had room for my wicker dining set.

He rolled his eyes and didn't say another word.

Twenty years later I had degenerated into a total mess by living with Michael and feeling worthless after losing my job. I had let clutter take over my spaces. Even my own living room."

It was time to make a change.

She realized Saturday morning that she'd had a complete breakthrough the day before. She was grateful that she recognized it in time. She was relieved she didn't have to ask God for a 2nd chance.

She had given herself another chance!! She was alive. The sun porch had saved her!!

Thank God!

She felt like Scrooge on Christmas morning having an awakening to a New Life.

It was her Project Manager mentality plus her belief in God that pulled her out of a serious depression.

She had analyzed her situation to Death. And Beyond.

Her mind had been racing since 6 am. When she checked on Sheridan she noticed he was still asleep.

After Sheridan woke up from the couch on the sun porch, Cheryl made breakfast of scrambled eggs with cheese and hashbrowns. They talked and laughed about the day before. Then he left for his house. Or Katherine's duplex. She wasn't sure where.

Cheryl remembered one of her Prospect Park Garden Club members ~ a woman named Debbie ~ was having an afternoon party in the neighborhood before taking off for Thailand to live for 2 years.

She went to the Garden party and loved seeing her neighbors. They had no idea that she almost killed herself the day before. She enjoyed the experience in a new light ~ realizing that she wouldn't be experiencing the backyard party if she had been dead.

She noticed everybody talking and laughing at the party. She tasted food that she never would have tasted if she'd killed herself.

For her, the Prospect Park garden party wouldn't have existed in her world.

It was a revelation! The party would have happened but she wouldn't have experienced it!

The neighbors wouldn't have found out about her death until much later. They would have wondered why she didn't show up to the Garden party when she said she'd be there. Some of them, like Mary Alice, may have felt a bit guilty. Mary Alice knew Cheryl had been depressed for quite some time. Mary Alice was a close friend to both Cheryl and Michael.

Cheryl spent the rest of the weekend working on the house. She took Baby Steps. Cleaning one thing at a time. Including weeding the overgrown garden. She did not get the house totally cleaned up but made great progress. By the time Michael got back Sunday night many things had changed in the house.

He said in amazement after he came back home and looked around, "What happened?!"

She said innocently, "I just needed time by myself to get stuff done."

She didn't go into details with Michael about her near suicide. She didn't want to worry him. After all, his sister tried to commit suicide and it was a very traumatic experience for him. He was still dealing with it almost 40 years later.

He had recently started talking about his sister's attempted suicide with friends after seeing the movie on DVD *'The Prince of Tides'* starring Barbara Streisand and Nick Nolte. He had gone on endlessly talking about how his friend, Angie, had helped him deal with the emotional backlog around his sister's trauma.

It was enough to make Cheryl feel really useless as a wife. Angie was the one he turned to for emotional support these days, not Cheryl anymore. Even though Angie was married to someone else, Cheryl still felt jealous of Michael's attention to her.

* * *

It was a few weeks after July 15 and the first part of August when Sheridan said to Cheryl while at Bally's working out at 5 am, "You know Cher, you are really different these days. You are no longer depressed. The cleaning thing on the sun porch really worked, didn't it?"

"Yup. It really did," she replied.

He noticed Cheryl was laughing all the time. Everything was funny to her.

Sheridan had a passion for watching movies so he suggested they watch the movie, *'What About Bob?'* starring Bill Murray and Richard Dreyfuss. He had a copy of it from the library.

Cheryl was not much for sitting still and watching movies with anybody, even her husband Michael, and ESPECIALLY not during the day when it was nice outside but she reluctantly agreed.

It took them 3 days to watch the movie. They started at Sheridan's house early in the mornings before their workouts. They watched part of the movie each day and then headed off to the Bally's fitness center.

After finally finishing the movie at 6 am on a Wednesday morning, Cheryl was howling with laughter. She said to Sheridan:

"I'm really Bob in this movie, aren't I? I'm all about having fun these days. I should be seeing a Psychiatrist after getting so close to killing myself. But I'm not. I'm just enjoying life. Just like Bob. Bill Murray as the character Bob is having the time of his life. He's the one driving his Psychiatrist nuts, played by Richard Dreyfuss."

The Psychiatrist even writes a book in the movie called, **"Baby Steps"**.

That's exactly what Cheryl had been doing every day since she started cleaning the sun porch on July 15.

Taking Baby Steps.

The morning they finished watching the movie they took off on Sheridan's motorcycle for their workout but stopped at the Manning's Café garden on Como Ave a few blocks away from his house.

It was Cheryl's idea to look at the beautiful wild flowers. As they were sitting on the garden bench appreciating the flowers and laughing about the *'What About Bob?'* movie, Sheridan's phone rang. It was his cousin Roger.

"I've got to go!" He said as he raced off. His cousin needed help delivering appliances at Menard's.

"Wait!!" Cheryl said as he was almost out of range. "What about going to the club this morning to work out? I thought that's what we were going to do after the movie?!"

He said he'd get back to her.

After he raced off on his motorcycle she realized she couldn't depend on Sheridan to be there for her. She needed to focus on her own life. She had driven over to his house that morning and she had her car with her. She wasn't worried about getting home.

She watched the butterflies for awhile in the Manning's garden and then noticed the dragonflies. They were just as beautiful as the butterflies.

She followed one particular dragonfly around the garden until it stopped and rested on the branch of a small tree. She was amazed that it blended perfectly with the branch.

As she got closer it didn't move. It completely stopped moving as if it was watching her. Its wings were motionless. It was frozen in Time.

She became fascinated.

She got closer. She looked at the dragonfly's eyes. Everything about the dragonfly had stopped moving. Except its eyes. They were rolling around looking at the environment. Including her.

She felt as if she was a little kid again.

In all her 57 years she had never really noticed dragonflies before. How could this be?? It was as if they were invisible to her. She wasn't afraid of them, just unaware of them.

She watched the Dragonfly not moving for at least 10 minutes (a long time) when her cell phone went off in her pocket. She took her phone out very slowly and carefully to see who was calling. It was Fran. Her friend from the University.

"Cheryl, do you have a minute? What are you doing?"

"Yes, Fran, I have a minute. I'm looking at a Dragonfly."

"What??"

"It's a long story, Fran. What's up?"

"Oh – it's about my husband Mel. He's giving me a hard time about this upcoming weekend going away with our friends. We just had an argument. You know what that's like."

"Yup, I know," said Cheryl.

Fran went on to describe in detail what was going on. Cheryl was listening but at the same time fascinated by watching the Dragonfly, which still hadn't moved.

At the end of Fran's story, Cheryl asked if there was anything she could do.

"Nope," said Fran. "Just listening was enough. Thanks!"

"OK."

She had another revelation.

Cheryl realized that if she were dead she never would have been there for Fran's call. Fran would have still been dealing with Cheryl's suicide.

She made a difference just by being there for Fran!

What a concept! If Fran only knew… Someday she'd tell her. But not now. Too much information to process. She hadn't told Fran anything about her near suicide.

Cheryl was living in the Now. In the Present Moment. Like she had never done before in all her Life.

Cheryl was pondering all of this when her cell phone rang again. She noticed it was Sheridan calling. He was apologizing for taking off so quickly after getting Roger's call. He offered to come back on his motorcycle to take her to her car.

"That's OK, Sher. I can walk to it. It's only a few blocks away and it's a beautiful morning. I've been studying Dragonflies here in the Manning's garden."

"What??!" He said. "What are you talking about?"

"I'll explain later. You keep working with your cousin Roger and I'll catch up with you."

TREA$URE YOUR LIFE | 65

Cheryl decided that Dragonflies were going to be her new passion. They were like Butterflies ~ and like her ~ always flying around from one thing to another. Cheryl was like that. But Dragonflies were different. They actually stopped and looked around. For a looonnnng time.

As if they were thinking.

Then they moved on flying about quickly. They seemed to have a purpose in life but Cheryl didn't know what it was. They were at least more intentional than Butterflies.

The sun was shining high in the sky on that August afternoon when Cheryl finally walked back to her car to head home.

Being unemployed did have its advantages. There was no schedule to adhere to and nobody cared where you were. Except maybe your Husband.

Michael worked from home as a Web Designer. He was always working it seemed. He had been doing this for many years ever since *he* had gotten laid off unfairly from his job at an enterprising internet company called MRNet.

It was why he completely sympathized with what Cheryl had gone through with her layoff from the U.

It has been said that **"A Players hire A Players, and B Players hire C Players."**

Cheryl first heard that phrase in a Management class at the Carlson School of Management within the University of Minnesota. She graduated with honors. It took her about 10 years. She had been working the whole time at the University and could only handle one class per quarter as a single parent after her divorce while raising her young daughter, Sarah.

Cheryl created the following extension which she quoted several times over the years:

"And C Players if they ever get into management positions through Freak Reorgs or Buyouts will not only lay off all the A Players, but they hire D Players. And then the company will turn to dust."

Cheryl created those phrases based on what she saw.

It happened to her husband's company and many others that she knew. Michael's company ~ MRNet ~ was an enterprising internet company that was growing quickly in the early 90's. They were comprised of highly intelligent people who really cared about non-profits and making access to the internet possible. MRNet stood for Minnesota Regional Network.

MRNet was bought by an established organization of 'old white guys' who looked at MRNet as a way to make some money.

The first thing the **C Players** did from the **Buyout** was to lay off all the **A Players** from MRNet (including the top strategic thinkers) and hire **D Players**. Michael was one of the upper management creative people, and so was his boss, the CEO and President.

Michael's layoff was sudden. Without any warning.

Fifteen years later the company was dust. Nobody was left. No pensions, no upper management, nothing.

In Cheryl's mind, the definition of an **A Player** was *not* that they were the most intelligent, but that they were Hard-Working,

Ethical, Honest and Focused. They knew how to get things done and motivate people. They had a sense of Humor. They believed in themselves and gave others encouragement to do their jobs. One of the most important characteristics of **A Players** is that they did *not* feel threatened or jealous of anybody else's accomplishments.

B Players were similar in that they also worked hard and were honest in their work, but they tended to not have as much confidence in themselves. They let themselves get distracted by opportunities to waste time and therefore were not as focused as A Players. **B Players** sometimes felt jealous of A Players' accomplishments and compared themselves to them, which is why they hired people of lesser qualifications: the **C Players**.

C Players were just as intelligent as A Players and B Players but **C Players** were more charmers and schmoozers than hard-working, honest employees. They didn't believe in themselves. They felt jealous and threatened of their counterpart A and B Players and often took credit for their coworker's accomplishments or ideas. They were mean at work. They talked about other people negatively behind their backs. **C Players** acted like ***Bullies*** at work and intimidated others. They were the first to leave work early in order to have a good time. Promotions came to **C Players** through their *relationships* at work, *not* by their accomplishments.

D Players had lost their focus and the ability to believe in themselves. They were no longer trying to do a good job and were only interested in getting by. They were characterized as having a 'bad attitude'. They would often *not* even do the *minimum* required for a job. Their interests were clearly outside of work. They only worked to gain some money to support their habits and partying life.

F Players had lost interest in life, themselves, everything.

All of the **A,B,C,D,F Player** explanation was Cheryl's personal analysis. It seemed to fit with what she experienced at work.

Cheryl knew her former boss at the U, the woman named Tari, was definitely a **C Player**.

After studying the Dragonfly and walking to her car, Cheryl's mind flashed back to watching Tari with Rod at a PeopleSoft conference in Las Vegas *before* Tari became Cheryl's boss.

The CIO ~ a guy named Stanley ~ had decreed throughout all of OIT (Office of Information Technology) that *only* those employees within OIT who were *presenting papers* at the conference could attend the Las Vegas PeopleSoft conference. Nobody else could go.

Cheryl worked hard on a PeopleSoft reporting project and was presenting a paper at the conference, as were a few others from her Payroll team on various other PeopleSoft projects. The conference was being held at the MGM Grand Hotel but the University of Minnesota OIT employees were told they had to stay at the Excalibur Hotel nearby. It was cheaper.

The Excalibur was close to the MGM Grand but still quite a walk. About a mile each day to get to the conference. Nobody was allowed to rent cars on the University's budget.

Cheryl and several others were shocked to find both Tari and Rod attending the conference, yet ***neither one*** of them were presenting papers! What were ***they*** doing there? They were ***both*** staying at the more expensive MGM Grand Hotel!

Tari and Rod walked in together every morning to the PeopleSoft conference and left together every afternoon. What did they think people thought of that?

Tari and Rod were looking like a couple. Rod was Tari's boss. He was married. She was divorced.

By hanging out together in Las Vegas at the PeopleSoft conference and never seen apart from each other, even at PeopleSoft evening functions, they were clearly causing many of the U of MN people to wonder what was going on.

They were the buzz of the conference, at least within the University of Minnesota employees.

When Tari was asked ahead of time by an administrative staff member who set up the travel arrangements why she insisted on staying at the MGM Grand, Tari replied, "Because I'm *special*, that's why. Just do it. Stanley will approve it."

On that day in August as Cheryl was studying the Dragonflies, Cheryl's mind flashed to the few weeks before Tari became Cheryl's boss.

One of the upper managers within the U, a woman named Marilyn from HR told Cheryl that she was extremely frustrated with Tari. Marilyn had been trying to arrange a meeting with Tari for 3 weeks to talk about problems with the web team, delays, and other issues.

Tari's web team had a reputation for being late with web projects by several months, as well as not showing up for meetings on time, not taking notes, not returning phone calls, and playing chess and computer games during the day. People from other departments were frustrated. The list was long.

Tari was part of the problem. She had been appointed the web team leader by Stanley. Tari rarely came to meetings on time and often did not return phone calls ~ even to department heads within the U. She was always running late it seemed.

Tari's web team was often in crisis mode with their software changes creating havoc in the Payroll and HR system. Cheryl was the PeopleSoft Manager of the Payroll and HR system and had to be aware of the changes Tari's team was making from the web side.

On the day of Marilyn and Tari's meeting to discuss these issues, Tari took the day off as a vacation day. Marilyn was furious.

The next time Marilyn talked to Tari she told her directly, "*You need to be more like Cheryl. Cheryl doesn't cancel meetings with me. Cheryl's team shows up for meetings on time. They even do status reports. Her team always meets their target date for projects. They are not 5 months late like your team is.*"

A week later Marilyn told Cheryl of this conversation with Tari in one of their regular private update meetings in Marilyn's office. Cheryl laughed and said, "How did Tari take that?"

Marilyn told her, "Not very well, actually."

Two weeks later Tari became Cheryl's boss through the Freak Reorganization.

Cheryl thought, "What the ---?!!"

How in the world did Tari get *promoted* after having such a questionable work record??

Tari was a **C Player**, that was fairly clear. All of a sudden her 'relationship' with her boss, Rod, became an issue.

Cheryl did some inside research through her many contacts within the U (a major Big-10 university with over 65,000 students) and found out Tari didn't even have a college degree.

How dumb was that?? College degrees were the product of Big-10 Universities and Tari didn't even have one!

Out of the blue, Tari became Cheryl's boss through a Freak Reorganization orchestrated by Rod. Tari couldn't even manage 20 web team people successfully and yet suddenly was in a newly created Director position managing more than 100 people!

Cheryl's previous boss, a guy named Mark, had been pushed off to the side in the reorganization chart and was now managing the Data Security folks. Mark Powell was a highly respected and distinguished manager with years of successful experience managing people. He also had an MBA (a Master's Degree in Business Administration).

Many people were noticing that Tari had a relationship with her boss Rod, that was questionable.

How could this crazy reorganization happen at a major Big 10 University?

Cheryl's ongoing questions to the U upper management after the Freak Reorganization occurred were: "How did Tari get in that POSITION as Director of 100 people WITHOUT a college degree??!"

"Was it because she was in another POSITION with Rod?!"

It got people's attention.

It became very embarrassing for the University of Minnesota's Human Resources (HR) personnel to admit that a web team leader could have gotten into a Director position *without a college degree.*

Even they couldn't explain it. It didn't follow the standard procedure. No job description was posted ahead of time for the new Director position. It was a position created by Rod through the Reorganization. The HR people were at a loss to explain to Cheryl how it could have happened. They were embarrassed to even talk about it.

Cheryl also had people check on Rod's degree. She found out he had a 4 year B.S. degree from St. Cloud State. A school with a reputation as a party school. Not known for their academics.

Even though Tari and Rod had become employees through Stanley's approval, they hadn't been at the University that long. They were relatively new and still acting like consultants with unlimited expense accounts.

Stanley, the CIO, did nothing about it.

One of the first meetings Tari had as the new boss over Cheryl did not go well.

Tari said, "Cheryl, I've been reviewing your HR file. I have access to it now that I'm the Director and I noticed that in your most recent review, Mark gave you an overall rating of 4. I want to downgrade you to a 3 and put that in your file instead. You don't deserve a 4."

Cheryl was shocked. She replied, "You CAN'T do that! I didn't even work for you then! Mark gave me a 4 and I deserve that! You can't change reviews that have already been completed!"

Tari replied with, "Sorry. I'm in charge now. I can do whatever I want."

The rating scale for yearly reviews was 1-5, with 5 being the highest. Cheryl had gotten ratings of 4 or 5 throughout her 24 years at the University. The ratings sometimes had been tied to merit increases in pay, but the most recent ratings from reviews had no effect on a person's salary due to the tight budget.

Since Tari's intention of downgrading Cheryl's review in the HR file had *no effect* on her salary, Cheryl could only assume it was to make her upset. Which it did.

Cheryl left feeling the meeting very defeated. What in the world was going on? How could this *totally incompetent* and *Bullying* woman suddenly be in charge of Cheryl's life?

The University had been such a great place to work. What happened?

What happens when incompetent and insecure people who apparently don't like themselves suddenly wind up in places of power? Is that what happened at Enron? A company that employed 20,000 people but in December of 2001 filed bankruptcy because of the actions of a few key managers at the top. Employees lost billions in pensions.

It also affected the entire Arthur Andersen accounting firm, which went down with Enron in the scandal.

Did those few people really let power go to their heads because they were **C Players**? Is that what ultimately destroyed the company and affected thousands of people's lives?

According to Bethany McLean and Peter Elkind in their book '***The Smartest Guys in the Room***': "The Enron scandal grew out of a steady accumulation of habits and values and actions that began years before and finally spiraled out of control." [1]

"Though few people complained about it before Enron fell, Ken Lay's behavior [the CEO] also betrayed a powerful sense of personal entitlement.... He gave Enron jobs and contracts to his relatives. He and his family used Enron corporate jets as if they owned them... At lunchtime when his meal arrived, his staff carefully unwrapped it, placed the food on fine china, and served him lunch on a covered silver platter." [2]

"The sense of entitlement... was shared by many at Enron, from Ken Lay to the secretarial staff... Hundreds of [Enron] deal makers made a habit of flying first class and staying in deluxe hotels; no one seemed to care." [3]

"It's enough to make you wonder about a lot of things. Is there a way to change the laws so that there isn't such an oxymoron as legal fraud? Or does the problem go deeper than mere laws can solve, to fundamental human failings of self-delusion, greed, and ego run amok?" [4]

Why don't people stop them? Why are they afraid to speak up?

Enron's out-of-control spending was one of the reasons the entire company went bankrupt. Not the only reason, but certainly a major factor.

Cheryl thought that the **The Smartest Guys in the Room** were really **C Players** who have become arrogant and high on their own perceived power. It has nothing to do with honesty, hard-work or ethics.

It has everything to do with greed and being unethical at work and using *relationships* to gain advancement.

She wondered these things on that day in August as she was studying the Dragonfly.

She remembered that she did her part to speak up and question Tari and Rod's actions about their wild spending of taxpayer's money. Their Enron-like behavior. She quoted that phrase to Stanley~ the CIO.

She said to Stanley on that fateful day in his office within Morrill Hall:

> *"Tari and Rod are acting like Enron upper management employees. They are arrogant and do not care how much money they are spending. They feel they are above any kind of rules or checks on their spending decisions. It is causing many within the University to question where OIT is getting money from all of a sudden.*
>
> *Marilyn, the Director from HR has been asking many questions of me such as: Why are Tari and Rod attending multiple PeopleSoft conferences in the same year?*
>
> *Why are they hiring so many consultants through contracts of $200,000 to keep under the Regent's radar? Why are they purchasing software we don't need? Why are they spending all this MONEY!!?"*

In addition, Cheryl told Stanley,

> *"Tari and Rod are having weekly meetings at 3 pm on Thursdays between the two of them at a local bar named Sally's ~ next to the University campus. It shows on both their Outlook calendars.*
>
> *Only those of us on Tari's management team have access to their calendars. I am one of them who can see where their meetings are and who they are with."*

It wasn't as if University employees couldn't go out to an occasional Happy Hour after work and enjoy drinks with their friends, it was that Tari and Rod were so blatant about having their weekly meetings at 3 pm at a local bar that it was on their calendars!! As if they didn't care what their image looked like.

Cheryl's experience with companies outside the University during the 2 years she was gone saw consultant's behavior very similar to Tari and Rod's. Their behavior had the kind of mentality that doesn't worry about expenses or how much dinners cost, or software, or hotels or conferences. It all goes on expense accounts and gets magically paid.

But private companies aren't spending taxpayer's money.

Tari and Rod were each making over $100,000 per year on taxpayer's money. A salary not even most professors at the University were pulling in at that time. Because they were all state employees, salaries were public knowledge.

Her concerns fell on deaf ears with Stanley. What hurt Cheryl the most during her layoff, the part that *really* devastated her was that she trusted Stanley, the CIO. She had known him for most of her 20 years at the U.

Cheryl felt like *'The Karate Kid'*. It was a well-known movie where a young boy is being picked on by his classmates. He was doing nothing to intimidate or criticize anybody around him. Yet, a Bully in the Schoolyard was picking on him for no reason.

Tari was the Bully in the Schoolyard. She was the one picking on Cheryl for no apparent reason.

It was Tari's bullying actions in the workplace that resulted in Cheryl going directly to Stanley ~ the CIO ~ with her concerns over Tari and Rod's excessive spending. After the Freak Reorg, Cheryl reported to Tari who reported to Rod who reported to Stanley, the CIO (Chief Information Officer).

Cheryl's mind went back to many years before her layoff, when Cheryl had a job as Senior Programmer Analyst within the University Computer Center.

Stanley knew she had won the top award at a national database conference in Chicago with her database design for the University's new telecommunications system many years before she got laid off.

She was given less than 1 week to design an entire database system to gather specific information on 18,000 phones covering over 400 buildings and off-campus locations.

Phone numbers, types of phones, dial or push buttons, multi-line or single line phones, locations within offices on campus and many other details were needed to order a completely revamped phone and data system from a new telecommunications vendor.

The penalty to the U of M for not ordering the specifics of the new phone system by a certain contract date was $50,000 a day.

She was told about the potential penalty amount to the University in the first meeting she got asked to attend by her boss's boss at the time. A guy named Yen who said they needed her to build a 'quick database'. He told her she was the only one who could do it. On such short notice.

Yen believed in her.

The initial meeting was with a Sr Vice President who was in charge of the Telecommunications Dept. It was a Tuesday morning at 9 am and the database design had to be completed and ready to go by the next Monday morning at 8 am.

On that day in August after studying the Dragonfly she remembered it was less than 1 week and 1 hour from when she first heard about it to design a complete database for specific information that hadn't even been identified yet on 18,000 phones.

She remembered, "THEY didn't even know what was to be included for the new phone system ordering process. That was part of the information gathering in order to design the database."

All of it to avoid a $50,000/day penalty to the University of Minnesota if not done in time.

A daunting task. For anybody.

Cheryl came through with the database design and reports in less than one week and it was successful. The data collection portion of the project took several months up until the contract deadline date. Cheryl managed all of it including teams of people gathering the data in over 400 buildings and off-campus locations, producing reports for all departments within the U.

The U of M did not have to pay any penalties because they made the deadline order date.

Stanley was a consultant on the telecommunications project long before he became the CIO. Stanley and Cheryl were in many meetings together as part of the major upgrade. That's how they met and how Stanley got to know her.

Cheryl presented a paper at an international conference in Chicago on the design of the database after the project was over, how she did it and the timeline she was under. The conference gave her the top award for managing so much detail quickly under a tight deadline. Her design made the utmost use of the database built-in characteristics.

Her career within the U of M took off after that.

Stanley also knew about the recognition given to the web registration system she was a leader on that had gotten national attention.

Stanley knew Cheryl had a network of people within the University and was able to motivate people.

Cheryl was known for her sense of Humor. She laughed often at work. She was always trying to make other people laugh, too. One of her bosses, Mark Powell told her that he could always tell where she was on the floor in WBOB (the building name) by her laughter.

Cheryl was the Director of the Student Information Systems area within OIT when she resigned on April Fool's Day, 5 years before her layoff. Things were going well with the web registration project. It was far more successful than anyone anticipated. They were all surprised when the local WCCO - TV News did a special Dimension report on it.

Students loved the fact they could register for classes through the web. It was easy, fun, and colorful. They were the first in the country to be able to do such a thing with so many links.

Not only could students register for classes online, they could link to where their classes were through maps of the U, find out what books to order at the Bookstore, link to Faculty information, course descriptions, and Financial Aid information. The University had over 400 buildings, so any help for students to find classes was greatly appreciated.

No more standing in long lines waiting to register for classes. The new web registration system was front page news for the Minnesota Daily ~ the official U of M newspaper. Cheryl was interviewed and quoted on the project in a front page article.

Cheryl's co-worker, a guy named Michael Handberg, was the brains behind it all. Cheryl helped make it happen. Cheryl knew people behind the scenes within OIT. She got them to work together to overcome all kinds of hurdles, both in technology and territory. Cheryl and Michael talked often and laughed hysterically together.

Michael was Smart. Which made him Funny.

Shortly after the success of the web registration system was realized, both Michael and Cheryl had an opportunity to present their project at a special conference in Indiana. At something called WebDev. Indiana University was hosting a conference for other universities to present what they were doing with web projects.

Cheryl and Michael demonstrated a live, online and production web registration system in front of 300-400 people. They actually registered for classes using the web interface they had developed. At the end of the presentation it was Cheryl's idea to plug in the 5-minute WCCO TV videotape of their project. Cheryl had to talk Michael into that one on the plane ride to Indiana. He didn't think anybody would care.

Cheryl had a marketing degree from the Carlson School of Management at the University of Minnesota. She also had an MIS emphasis (Management Information Systems).

She told him on the plane, "Trust me, Michael. They're going to care that we have this videotape of our project. I'm in Marketing. I know."

Michael was the Brain. She was the Marketer.

The crowd was amazed. A couple of PeopleSoft representatives were in the crowd. They came up to Michael and Cheryl after their presentation and said, "You guys are already *doing* what we only have on paper and in diagrams for web registration! This is amazing! Can we talk?"

The TV video helped. It validated what they were doing.

The rest was history. PeopleSoft and the University of Minnesota became partners in the Student Information Systems area.

Stanley called her into his office in Morrill Hall and tried to persuade her to stay after he found out she resigned on April 1st. Five years *before* her ultimate layoff. April Fool's Day. Nobody believed her. Even Yen, her boss at the time, thought she was kidding.

Cheryl told Stanley and Yen after she resigned on April Fool's Day five years before her layoff that she wasn't kidding about leaving. She told them she wanted to move on and experience life *outside* the University.

Stanley and Yen continued to try and talk her into staying at the University after she resigned.

The *real* reason Cheryl resigned on April 1st had nothing to do with wanting to move on and experience life outside the University. Cheryl loved her life at the University of Minnesota.

Not only did she work there as an Information Technology Manager, she had graduated with honors from the Carlson School of Management and was in the honors group within CLA (College of Liberal Arts) before transferring to CSOM. Learning was something she truly enjoyed doing. The University was the perfect setting for her. It promoted continuous learning.

She had a network of friends. She met her husband Michael there. The University of Minnesota was her whole Life.

But Cheryl was being attacked and criticized by another powerful woman within the University community. The more successful the web registration project became, the more Cheryl got attacked verbally by the other woman.

The other woman, Barbara, was acting like a Bully. Barbara was the business side Director of Student Systems. Cheryl was the computer side Director of the same systems.

Cheryl remembered that if it wasn't for Barbara's inspiration and leadership in the database community, Cheryl never would have had the courage to present a paper at an international database conference in Chicago.

Many years before, Barbara had been President of the System 2000 User's Group. While President, she presented a paper on the University of Minnesota's System 2000 database design for the Admissions and Records student applications at a conference in Montreal, Canada. It was a successful and interesting presentation. A huge hit.

Cheryl was there to see it.

It was Cheryl's first and only database conference she had ever attended before presenting a paper in Chicago many years later. Barbara took Cheryl under her wing and guided her while in Montreal. She introduced Cheryl to people. She was the older, wiser mentor who opened doors for her in a sense.

They met on the plane flying from Minneapolis to Montreal. Cheryl recognized Barbara and introduced herself.

At that time, Cheryl was a Senior Analyst Programmer within the UCC Computer Center. She was selected to attend the database conference because she was good at answering questions on the System 2000 database Help-Line within the University.

Cheryl also created and taught a 3-week short course on the design of databases using the University's System 2000 software. She taught the class once per quarter for a few years. The software package was available on the mainframe computer system and used by thousands of people.

Over the years Barbara and Cheryl got to know each other better through many meetings at the University. The meetings occurred when the Admissions and Records Office had to update their computer applications. A continuous process. Updating computer systems and applications. Anybody involved with the computer world knows what that is like.

Cheryl's career path took her on a journey of managing projects and people within UCC until she was promoted to Director of Student Information Systems. Barbara was Director of the same systems on the business side. Within Admissions and Records.

In the big picture, Barbara became Cheryl's main client. Barbara was the 'Customer'.

Over time, Barbara became very protective of her territory on the business side of student systems and did not want the web efforts accessing *'her student data'*. Yet Barbara's boss, Bob Kvavik, totally supported the web registration project. Michael Handberg also reported directly to Bob Kvavik.

Cheryl was caught in the middle of the battle. Cheryl reported to Yen on the computer side of the house.

Over time Cheryl couldn't ignore the verbal attacks and criticism for being successful at web registration in Barbara's eyes. Barbara created public scenes in meetings and berated Cheryl for all of OIT's shortcomings. The public scenes hurt Cheryl emotionally.

Cheryl had looked up to Barbara so often over the years as a mentor that it was just too painful to be on the other end of Barbara's anger.

So one day, Cheryl gave up trying to deal with it all.

She started looking for another job and when she found one, she picked April Fool's Day as her resignation day. She figured nobody would believe her. They'd all think it was one of her jokes.

But the Joke would be that it was No Joke. She thought that was Funny.

Cheryl told Stanley and Yen all about her frustrations over being attacked for a successful project. They both knew. Their advice was to tell her to ignore the verbal attacks from Barbara and not worry about them. Barbara was not part of the OIT information technology department so they could do nothing about her.

Their advice did not help Cheryl to deal with being criticized for a successful project. She decided to leave the U anyway.

The University threw her a big party before she left. Michael Handberg, Stanley the CIO, and Bob Kvavik (Sr Vice President from the U) were at her going away luncheon. So was Barbara (the Bully) and about 100 other people.

TREA$URE YOUR LIFE | 85

Cheryl got an email that morning from the University's President, a guy named Nils Hasslemo. She was absolutely floored when she got that. How did *he* know she was resigning?

The email from Nils Hasslemo thanked her for all she did for the successful web registration at the U. She didn't do it all, though. She just connected people to make it happen. Michael Handberg was the brains behind the outfit.

Cheryl remembered on that August day studying dragonflies how much fun she'd had at her going away party from the U. Her husband Michael had arranged for and secretly flown up her daughter from Florida.

Towards the end of Cheryl's resignation speech in front of the crowd Cheryl was announcing where she was going saying, "Maybe I should go to... "

Sarah appeared from a door in the back of the room saying loudly, "FLORIDA!! MOM maybe you should go to FLORIDA!!"

Sarah took over the microphone as Cheryl was reduced to tears at seeing her Daughter. She was sobbing. The love of her life had just appeared again.

Ah yes, quite the going away party.

She left the U and pursued other job opportunities but was talked into going back after being gone for 2 years because she was needed for a PeopleSoft upgrade. Cheryl loved the University community.

What Cheryl realized while she was gone was that the camaraderie and commitment she experienced during her 20 years at the

University of Minnesota was unbelievably *high* compared to the 2 companies she worked at *outside* the U.

She went from people who had 100% commitment within an organization to those who had about 10%. In both companies outside the University the employees acted as if they were in a revolving door.

Outside the U, there was no camaraderie, no commitment, no laughter at work, nothing but turmoil and chaos. People were constantly coming and going ~ in and out of the organization. There was no institutional memory of projects and clients that she experienced at the University.

She hardly got to know anybody because nobody really knew anybody.

She was ready to go back to a more stimulating and cutting edge environment. Like the University of Minnesota. Where people were committed to doing a good job and performing at their best because they were **A Players** working with their friends. Where the Carlson School of Management within the University had an excellent reputation as a business school.

What nobody knew except her closest friends was that the week *after* Cheryl left the U, Barbara and Cheryl had lunch together. It was Barbara's idea. Barbara found out why Cheryl had resigned on April Fool's Day and wanted to get more information.

Barbara was very upset about it. Angry, in fact.

In an intense lunch conversation, the two worked out their differences.

Barbara started off the meeting by saying, "Do you know how much guilt you've put on me!?? Knowing I'm the reason you left? How could you DO that to me?!!"

Cheryl was stunned but a voice inside her head said, "Wait a minute. What is she going to do to me? FIRE ME?!! I've already QUIT! SHE can't to anything to me now. Besides I didn't even work for her. I worked for Yen. We already had the going away party. I'm gone. I'm not afraid of her anymore."

After thinking about it, Cheryl proceeded to rattle off a series of incidents where Barbara had publicly humiliated Cheryl.

She told Barbara with an intense amount of anger that surprised even herself, "Do you know what you SAID to me at that All-Campus managers meeting up in Duluth?!! Do you realize after the meeting I was in tears and cried most of the way home because I couldn't do anything about our rates in OIT? Or any of the other issues you had with us?? Or web registration which was already well under way by that time? You were taking it all out on me!!"

Barbara softened for a moment and then had tears in *her* eyes when she realized how much hurt she had caused Cheryl.

She said to Cheryl, "Why didn't you come to me? Why did you stuff all your feelings over these years? Why didn't you let me know what you were going through?!"

It was Cheryl's turn to soften. She replied, "You know, it didn't even occur for me to do that. You were the Customer. The Customer is always right. Right?"

On that day during lunch at that moment they both realized that if Cheryl had taken the initiative and gone to Barbara directly with her concerns, Cheryl would *not have quit* on April Fool's Day.

Barbara admitted, "I thought you were as tough as nails, Cheryl. I didn't think anything I said bothered you. I had no idea I was hurting you so much."

In one lunch, the two became friends again.

Barbara was no longer the Bully. She turned back into a Friend.

Through yet another series of reorganizations over the 2 years Cheryl was gone, Barbara wound up reporting directly to Stanley ~ the CIO. Barbara called Cheryl one weekend at home and asked her to come back to the University for a PeopleSoft upgrade project.

Barbara was instrumental in bringing Cheryl back to the U. Cheryl was rehired immediately.

Within a month after Cheryl was hired back, Barbara left the University for a lucrative consulting job at Coopers & Lybrand. So did Michael Handberg. They both wound up at the same place not knowing each other had quit the same week.

Cheryl thought that was Funny. Actually Hilarious.

Just as Cheryl was coming back to the U, her two long-time comrades who were always doing battle with each other were quitting. They were both leaving the University. And yet were landing at the same place. She wondered if their battles were going to continue.

The Universe works in mysterious ways, she remembered thinking. So does the University!

This was why 3 years after Cheryl came back she went to Stanley ~ the CIO ~ with her concerns over Tari's wild spending of taxpayer's money. Both her allies Barbara and Michael Handberg were gone. Tari had been promoted to Michael Handberg's role as web team leader by Stanley after Michael left the U.

To her surprise, Stanley did nothing. Except look uncomfortable at the end of their meeting. He told her he was flying that weekend to New Orleans with Tari to attend another PeopleSoft conference.

Cheryl's heart sank as he told her this. She wound up on the layoff list immediately after that.

Stanley has since left the University. Cheryl heard through her many contacts at the U that he went to some university in Florida.

On that August day studying the Dragonfly, Cheryl remembered how she fought back after her layoff.

Tari and Rod's legal argument during the layoff was that Cheryl did not have enough years of seniority in her management position of the PeopleSoft Payroll team. During a Budget Crisis, those at the lowest level of seniority were to be laid off.

Tari's claim was that Cheryl had *only* been working at the University for 3-½ years. Tari knew about Cheryl's previous 21 years although they hadn't actually worked together. During the time Cheryl was quitting as Director of Student Information Systems, Tari was being hired as a web programmer under Michael Handberg, the web team leader.

The question raised by Cheryl during the legal grievance was: "Why were there layoffs during a Budget Crisis in the Information Technology Department when Tari in her new position as Director assured her own management team there was going to be *no* layoffs?"

Tari told her leadership team the week BEFORE any layoffs occurred that ALL budget problems were going to be solved through attrition, closing unfilled job positions, and cutting expenses. Cheryl brought this up during the U of M legal grievance process.

Both Tari and Rod attempted to cover up the fact Cheryl had been *fully reinstated* when she was hired back at the University after being gone for 2 years. Cheryl had MORE seniority than anybody else in her management position as the PeopleSoft HR and Payroll leader ~ 24-½ years of seniority to be exact.

She even had more seniority than Ann, her counterpart PeopleSoft manager and close friend.

Ann and Cheryl compared notes after the layoff. They still talked almost every day on the phone ~ like some sisters do. They both knew who had more seniority. Both of them had quit the University years before and were gone for a short period of time before being hired back with full reinstatement seniority.

If anybody had to be laid off during Budget Cuts at a particular PeopleSoft manager's level, it should have been Ann. It was close, but Cheryl had more seniority by about 6 months. They both knew it.

Tari and Rod modified the official rehire letter that Cheryl had gotten 3 years before and had *taken out* the lines that gave Cheryl full reinstatement of her seniority of over 20 years, plus her vacation earning and her sick leave bank of 400 hours.

A draft of the HR letter was still in Cheryl's official HR file. Tari as the new Director, had access to Cheryl's file.

Tari and Rod showed up at the U of M legal grievance proceedings with a white sheet of paper that had the date of her rehire letter and the exact words typed on it, but *without* the reinstatement lines.

The lines and words describing in detail about the reinstatement were missing. The letter was unsigned.

Cheryl showed up at the same legal grievance proceedings with a signed letter from her rehire boss, a woman named Kris, on official University of Minnesota letterhead with maroon and gold colors at the top. It clearly stated all the terms of the reinstatement.

Kris was no longer working at the U, but Cheryl contacted her before the legal grievance hearing. Kris agreed to testify in person if necessary and validate that Cheryl was fully reinstated with all years of seniority at the time of rehire.

At the internal legal hearing with the Grievance Officer named Carolyn, Cheryl had one of her bowling buddies representing her as a legal counsel from the Civil Service Committee: a guy named Blake. Blake was on her U of M softball team. And her U of M bowling team.

Tari and Rod must have thought Cheryl lost the original signed letter on University letterhead.

Both Tari and Rod looked like Idiots with their unsigned letter that had the reinstatement lines missing. Blake was a witness. Carolyn the Grievance Officer, rolled her eyes.

Cheryl won the legal grievance easily after that.

Cheryl got a *lot* more money than the 3 weeks pay originally offered in her severance letter from Tari. The 3 weeks pay amount was standard severance pay in layoff situations: 1 week of pay for each year of service. Tari had offered 3 weeks of severance pay for what Tari claimed was Cheryl's 3 years of University service.

After Cheryl won the legal grievance and was able to prove that she had 24 ½ years of seniority and therefore should *never* have been laid off during a Budget Cut when at least one person at her manager level had less seniority, Cheryl called Tari on the phone to ask if she could get her job back.

She called early one morning and happened to catch Tari in her office. In an awkward conversation, Tari hesitated nervously and told Cheryl she'd get back to her after checking with Stanley.

The next day Tari called Cheryl back to tell her that Stanley and Tari talked it over and decided that the situation between Cheryl and Tari was too 'toxic' for Cheryl to return.

Cheryl wondered if Tari discussed the matter with Stanley at all.

But at that point, Cheryl had to agree that the situation was indeed toxic between the two of them and would probably never be the normal manager / employee relationship one would expect from a respected Big 10 institution. Cheryl had *no respect* for Tari as a manager after all she had been through.

In addition, Cheryl figured that Tari would be constantly criticizing and undermining everything Cheryl attempted to do, no matter what the task was. Tari had started doing that to Cheryl even *before* her layoff.

After Cheryl called Tari and tried to get her job back, Ann (the other PeopleSoft manager and close friend of Cheryl's) decided that she'd had enough of Tari and Rod. Ann was upset with the way Cheryl had been treated by Tari, Rod and Stanley. Ann knew about the phone call and had even encouraged Cheryl to call Tari to try and get her job back.

Ann also knew that Cheryl had gone to Stanley in January to express her concerns over excessive spending of taxpayer's money by Tari and Rod. Ann knew how Cheryl had been forced to leave the University and how she had suffered emotionally. Ann and Cheryl were still very close friends.

Ann told Cheryl in a phone call, "I've had it with all of them. I can no longer work for people who are so unethical. I've decided to take an early retirement from the U and stay home to take care of my new Granddaughter. With you gone, Cheryl, there is no enjoyment or satisfaction for me anymore at the U. It has become a dreadful job. I hate it there. Things have changed so much. The current leadership is not one I can get behind."

In a surprise move to everybody, Ann quit years before she planned to and took an early retirement. The U gave her a big going-away luncheon party which Cheryl attended on Ann's invitation. Cheryl completely avoided interacting with Tari at Ann's sendoff.

Cheryl moved on and started looking for another job but not before contacting the Office of Internal Audits within the University and requesting an internal audit of OIT's (Office of Information Technology) expenses, including all travel and consultant's contracts. Her friends from the Audit office updated her on the progress of the internal audit.

She got the satisfaction of knowing both Tari and Rod were walked out the door several months later.

By the time Tari and Rod were gone from the University, Cheryl was working as a Project Manager in a completely different organization.

Cheryl continued to bowl on the University Bowling League after her layoff. The U of M bowling league had been bowling at the Midway Pro Bowl on Snelling and University Avenue for over 30 years, right next to Rainbow Foods. Cheryl not only knew just about everyone on the league, she knew Scott, the Pro Bowl Manager.

Scott was Funny which made him Smart. He always made her laugh.

It was a fun league. Bowling gave her access to inside information of what was happening within her former department. She knew that the worker bees within the U in all departments had an amazing amount of information. And she found out a LOT more from these worker bees after they'd had a few beers.

Weedo was one of the many co-workers who helped her find answers to what was going on. So did Jaimie who's nickname was Aime. Plus bowlers from the Human Resources Dept, the Civil Service Committee and the Internal Audit group. Bowlers were great sources of information.

She also got inside information from Mike, whose bowling nickname was Woe ~ her close friend from the U.

She found it Funny that even after she had gotten laid off, she knew more details of who had quit the U, who had gotten promoted, who was getting married, who was pregnant and who was getting divorced than most people that still worked there. She stayed in touch with her former colleagues by having lunches with them.

Marilyn, the Director from HR told her at one of their lunches after Cheryl left the U, "How do you know so much about what is going on? You don't even work there anymore! You know more than I do."

Cheryl replied, "Because I still bowl with lots of people that work there. And I talk to them a lot. They tell me stuff. That's how I know."

Marilyn laughed and said, "Maybe I should start bowling so I can find out what's going on in my OWN department!"

The unfairness of being laid off for reporting their Enron-type behavior still crossed Cheryl's mind from time to time.

On that day in August when Cheryl studied the Dragonfly, she finally made peace with the entire situation.

What goes around comes around... they say. People who are inept or are **C Players** and mistreat others really don't last long in an organization. If they remain in charge, the organization doesn't last long. They hire **D Players** and the company turns to dust.

She wasn't sure where Tari or Rod or Stanley were outside the University, but Cheryl's life sure had changed dramatically.

"If Tari hadn't laid me off unfairly because of her relationship with Rod and her jealousy of my PeopleSoft projects and successful web registration at the U, I wouldn't be here. I wouldn't have noticed Dragonflies. I wouldn't have noticed life itself.

I would be unappreciative of my life.

"I would be working at a management job at the University knowing that the rest of my life was probably set. I would not have to worry about anything except getting the next project done. I would be waiting for retirement. I would not notice the warm sun shining on this beautiful day in August.

I would not really be living."

The thought of thanking Tari for laying her off crossed her mind briefly. But she decided not to pursue that.

She knew people who would know how to get ahold of Tari. She had heard Tari was in some other state – Colorado or California. One of those 'C' states. It figured. Tari was a **C Player** after all.

Cheryl chuckled to herself. These days everything was amusing to her.

"I'm sure there are some very smart **A Players** who live in those 'C' states. Tari's just not one of them."

As she drove home with renewed energy she realized just how alive she was. She could have been dead. Her husband, Michael, could have been still dealing with the aftermath of her funeral on a day she was driving home in the morning after her workout to see him.

He had no idea what she was going through.

She was very much alive!

Chapter 4 ~ The Argument

It was a few weeks after July 15. The first week in August. Cheryl drove home after discovering Dragonflies at the Manning's garden for the first time in her life. She was awake to everything now. The blue sky. The warm sun. The colorful flowers in her garden as she drove up to her Prospect Park house.

The Dragonfly she had just stopped to study.

As she arrived home she noticed how much cleaner and organized the house was. It still had Michael's newspapers and clutter in *his* living room but she no longer felt overwhelmed. *Her* living room was clean. The kitchen was clean. Even the floor was clean and waxed. The garden in front was weeded so that the flowers came through in magnificent colors.

The sun porch was magical with the morning sun shining through it.

Cheryl went to the sun porch immediately to enjoy the early sun shining through it. The rays took her breath away. Now that it was clean she could look out through the windows to the back yard.

It was amazing! Even in the heart of Minneapolis the plant life within Prospect Park was incredible. Their back yard looked like a forest within the city.

She took a few breaths at the beauty of the back yard. She was grateful to be alive. She realized if she were dead, she never would have seen the garden like that.

It was another revelation! Just being able to look at the garden and the back yard on that day was a wonder to her.

She went upstairs to find Michael in the bathroom. She initiated a conversation with him about everyday stuff people talk about when they are married. She felt happy and confident.

Before she knew it, he started an argument with her. She was caught unaware. As she usually was.

This time she didn't react like she had for the last 20 years. She did not back down and become docile and loving in order to pacify his inappropriate anger. She often reacted to his quickly escalating anger with softening responses to try and calm him. Either that or she left the scene if he was too Angry.

She told her close friends that Michael's anger went off as quickly as striking a match. Without ANY warning.

Michael suddenly changed the tone of the conversation that fateful morning by screaming at her, "And you DESTROYED my relationship with Angie!!"

To which Cheryl replied with an intensity of anger she had never experienced in her life. She was born and raised Lutheran and rarely raised her voice, but she did that day.

She SCREAMED BACK at the top of her lungs as if she was on a roller coaster at Valley Fair:

"I LOVE YOU!!! I HATE THIS CLUTTER YOU HAVE IN THIS HOUSE!!! YOU THINK I DESTROYED YOUR RELATIONSHIP WITH ANGIE? HOW DO YOU THINK I FELT WHEN YOU LIED TO ME ABOUT NOT MEETING WITH HER, WHEN YOU REALLY DID!! HOW DO YOU

THINK I FELT ABOUT SEEING YOU TWO TOGETHER??? I HATE YOUR NEWSPAPERS!!! I CAN'T LIVE LIKE THIS ANYMORE. I'M GOING FOR A WALK! I'LL BE BACK LATER!"

The woman called Angie in Michael's life was a married woman he had fallen in love with. Hopelessly. Over the last 8 years ~ ever since they worked together at MRNet. The same company Michael later got laid off from. The same company that turned to dust after the **C Players** took over from the **Buyout**.

Michael told his friends that Angie was similar in many ways to Rachel, his 7th grade girlfriend, who was the only one in Michael's early life who gave him credit for his amazing intelligence. Rachel was cute, smart, tall and a long-haired brunette.

Just like Angie.

Michael had gotten to know Angie by making the effort to have lunch or coffee with her over the years since they stopped working together at MRNet. Because Angie was married to someone else, at first Cheryl didn't worry about his coffee meetings with her.

Until she suspected that maybe something else was going on.

Angie was definitely the most attractive of all Michael's female friends. And the smartest. She had a Master's Degree from Berkeley. Michael had a Master's Degree from the University of Minnesota. Cheryl only had a Bachelor's degree from the Carlson School of Management at the U of M and often felt stupid around them. She wondered if Angie's husband felt the same.

Michael loved talking about philosophical stuff on his coffee meetings with Angie. Ken Wilbur. Quantum physics. Both Michael and Angie had paying jobs. Both their spouses had gotten laid off and were unemployed. Angie's husband was an Architect who had gotten laid off in the faltering economy. Gary drank a lot. Cheryl had been known to drink a lot, too.

Neither Michael nor Angie were affected by alcohol. They didn't drink, didn't smoke and even looked somewhat alike.

Michael kept telling Cheryl that his friendship with Angie was 'strictly platonic'. Nothing was going on. They were 'just friends'.

Cheryl ran across an email on the printer she shared with Michael in January of that year that listed Panera Bread as a meeting location between the two of them on a Saturday afternoon from 2 to 4 pm. That particular day she had asked Michael what his plans were and he did not tell her he was meeting Angie for coffee in the afternoon. He had always told her before that.

She decided to show up to see what their meetings were like.

While Cheryl was in the background getting coffee at Panera Bread, she watched the two of them. They were both oblivious to everything surrounding them in a crowded coffee shop. They were sitting next to a window on a cold gray January day in a Panera Bread near Hopkins.

Cheryl was heartbroken as she watched her Husband laugh and explain excitedly to Angie some articles he had in a vanilla folder. Angie was also similarly interested in what he was saying.

Cheryl thought to herself as her stomach tied up in knots, "He used to look at me like that. He used to laugh and explain stuff to me just like he is doing with her now. He would tell his friends that our relationship was 'strictly platonic'. That was way before we became romantically involved. He doesn't do that with me now.

He doesn't seem to laugh and enjoy my company anymore, it seems."

She watched them from a distance for as long as she could stand it before she left and went home.

She waited for him and shortly after she got there, Michael showed up. She asked him where he had been. He looked away from her and said somewhat vaguely, "I decided to stop in at Panera Bread on Excelsior and get a Ceasar salad after my workout. That's it."

After a few minutes of casual conversation while Cheryl was trying to be cool, she asked him if he had been with Angie. He looked startled and said, "No. Absolutely not! Why did you ask that?"

Cheryl felt embarrassed that she had watched them so she dropped the issue.

A few days later she brought it up again and said, "Michael it just seems weird that you would stop at a Panera Bread after your workout and get a Ceasar salad. That is so unlike you. Besides, that Panera Bread is out of the way from your training session with Steven and our house. It doesn't make sense."

It was at that point that he admitted he had met Angie on Saturday afternoon. When she asked him why he didn't say that right away, he said, "Because you are starting to get jealous of me seeing her and I didn't want to upset you."

Cheryl never told him that she had seen him at Panera Bread. She still felt embarrassed that she actually stayed and watched them without saying anything. So he had no idea she knew.

A few weeks later in February Cheryl discovered another email on the printer for a coffee meeting with Angie at a Dunn Bros in

Linden Hills. As he was leaving that Saturday morning for errands and his workout, Cheryl asked him where he was going that day. He said nothing about meeting Angie even when she asked him if he was going to meet her. He denied it and made something up.

The email Cheryl had discovered on the printer said something about sharing their most treasured and best times together that happened between the two of them. It was Michael's idea. Michael called it 'Their Top 10 list.'

This time Cheryl agonized about it all afternoon at home. What should she do? She knew where and when they were meeting but didn't want to go through the pain of watching her Husband act so delighted and fascinated with another Woman. Even if it was at a coffee shop.

It was too painful. Especially since he used to do that with Cheryl. She knew what it was like for him to find *her* fascinating and enchanting, listening to her and hanging on her every word.

She attempted to distract herself with computer games at home. It didn't work. She told herself to just stay there and ask Michael about it when he came home. Like the other time at Panera Bread.

But at some point as the clock was ticking and she couldn't help but watch the time on her computer, she finally gave in.

She told herself, "Angie needs to know that he's lying to me. She is an intelligent and respectable woman. I actually like her. She's nice to me and seems to have integrity. If I were in her situation, I'd sure like to know that the guy I'm meeting for coffee and conversation is a Liar."

So she headed out the door quickly knowing their coffee meeting was coming to an end. She remembered thinking, "This could dramatically affect our marriage. But at this point I don't care. He doesn't find me interesting anymore anyway."

Cheryl said to the both of them as she walked into the Dunn Brothers coffee shop on a gray February Saturday afternoon, "Is there something going on here that I should know about?"

Angie was very calm and relaxed as she said, "Hi Cheryl. How are you?"

Michael appeared a bit nervous.

Cheryl was very agitated and told Angie that Michael had lied to her the last 3 times he met for coffee with Angie. He had been denying he was even seeing Angie at all.

Angie turned to Michael and was furious. She said to him, "You LIED to her about us meeting for coffee???? Why???!"

Angie left in a huff. She had *not* been lying to her husband about meeting Michael for coffee at a Dunn Brothers in Linden Hills.

So, why was Michael lying to his wife???

It was the end of their coffee meeting relationship. Angie ended it shortly afterwards with an email.

This is what Michael had been harboring for 6 months when he blew up at Cheryl and said on that fateful day in August, "YOU DESTROYED MY RELATIONSHIP WITH ANGIE!!"

Actually, it was the first time Michael admitted to Cheryl that his *'friendship'* with Angie was really a *'relationship'*.

He kept telling Cheryl that there never had been any physical contact between him and Angie. No hugging. No kissing. No sex. What was she worried about?

Cheryl knew that an Emotional High with no sex between two people could often be more powerful than if a physical relationship existed. At least with sex there is orgasm and a finish. Without sex, there is *no end* to the Emotional Fantasy.

Cheryl stormed out and went for a walk in the neighborhood while Michael went for a bike ride around Lake Calhoun. Both were extremely agitated.

Michael's agitation was normal. Cheryl's was *not*.

Cheryl was furious over his sudden outburst. It wasn't the first time he had done that. She had no patience anymore for his temper tantrums. She was also furious at herself for reacting so strongly to him screaming at her.

She headed for her friend Lori's house a block away. Lori would know what to say to her. Lori knew all about what had been going on lately, even Cheryl's near suicide.

As Cheryl approached Lori's house, she saw that the French doors to Lori's house on the garden side were closed. It was a sign Lori was not home. Lori loved being in her garden and was often outside moving plants around and weeding her adorable Prospect Park Garden. If the doors were open, Lori was home.

Cheryl knocked on the closed doors but was right. No answer. Lori was gone.

By knocking on the doors Cheryl discovered Lori's beautiful white cat named Ming sitting outside under the patio furniture.

She knelt down next to Ming and sat down on the patio stone. Cheryl started crying. She picked Ming up and held him in her lap. What a beautiful *extremely* long-haired white cat Ming was!! Cheryl petted and held him for a long time, hidden from the rest of the world by the tall Zinnias and white Lilies in Lori's garden.

She wanted to talk to someone but forgot to bring her cell phone. The only thing she could do was talk to Ming. Which she did.

After an hour she calmed down and gradually started walking back the other way around the block.

She arrived home at exactly the same minute Michael did from his bike ride. Both of them were calmed down. Cheryl had decided during her walk in the neighborhood that she needed to get away from him for awhile. She no longer had patience for his Rage and inappropriate Anger.

She felt like a kicked dog.

Cheryl had grown up in a very loving Lutheran family. Michael had not. His first wife, Carol, also grew up in a loving Lutheran family. Both Cheryl and Carol played the piano. So did Annabel, Michael's live-in girlfriend after his divorce.

Somehow, Michael had been drawn to women who played the piano. Women who played fairly well, in fact.

Cheryl accused him several times over their 20 year marriage of taking out his Rage from his abusive family system on her. She said many times that she was *not* in this world to take on the abuse of his family and his Father. And his father's Father. She did not deserve that.

She also accused him of being addicted to his own Rage. He seemed to get off on getting very angry and explosive, then calming down and apologizing. It was as if the adrenalin rush was what he craved. He neither drank nor took any other drugs. He got off on getting off.

Rage was his drug.

Michael had taken Anger Management classes years before when Cheryl threatened to leave him. The classes worked for awhile but then he gradually resorted to exploding quickly like a lit match.

Cheryl finally became strong enough to take a different type of action after her experience on July 15. She was alive. She could have been dead.

Instead of dealing with the after effects of her funeral, Michael was dealing with Cheryl being very much alive.

He had no idea what was happening to her. Cheryl never told him about her July 15 experience. She didn't want to worry him that she had come so close to suicide.

Cheryl announced to Michael after they both got back from their respective time outs on that fateful day in August that she wanted to go to Alabama starting the next day to attend a church retreat about Goal Setting. It was offered by a Unity minister named Edwene Gaines who had spoken at her Unity Church in Golden Valley two weeks before.

It was something she had been pondering for a week. Michael told her she was crazy. How would she pay for it?

He told her bluntly, "You have NO job!"

"I'll come up with the money somehow. I'll take my car go to Chicago the first night to spend with Dad. Then I'll figure out the rest. I need to get to Alabama by Friday night."

She took her large glass jar similar to a piggy bank and counted all the money. It totaled $80. That was enough for gas, she figured. She had a dependable Toyota Corolla.

She took the rest of the money for the weekend from her dwindling savings, and through a web site secured a bed and breakfast in Mentone, Alabama for 3 days.

She was all set.

She was not going to take any more inappropriate abuse from Michael for anything. She was done with that. She was just as strong and confident as when she first married him. He was taken aback.

He was unable to control her anymore. He married her for her confidence and now after 20 years was facing the same confident woman he married. Somewhere during their marriage, she lost herself.

Cheryl took off on Thursday afternoon from Minneapolis for a Friday weekend retreat in Alabama. Approximately 1,000 miles. She called Sheridan and told him he'd be working out by himself at Bally's for a couple of days.

He was very surprised by her sudden decision, but supported her and said, "Good luck, Cher. Keep in touch."

It was the Beginning of the End.

Of the next chapter in her life.

Chapter 5 ~ Discovering Tree Frogs

Cheryl drove to Chicago on what she thought would be a non-event as the first part of getting to Alabama. Chicago was 400 miles away. She had been making this trip from Minneapolis to Chicago for the last 35 years -- ever since her dad had gotten promoted to a Land O' Lakes Regional Director.

She knew the trip well. Taking freeway I-94 from Minneapolis to his home in Naperville was not a big deal for her.

This trip was different.

Her intention was to take off early Thursday morning but because she had decided only the day before to leave for a major trip to Alabama it took her longer to get ready than she planned.

She didn't leave until almost 3 pm Thursday afternoon.

This type of impulsive decision-making drove her dad nuts. He was a Planner. He never did anything quite as spontaneous as his daughter did unless someone died. Even in those cases he usually had a couple of days warning.

Cheryl kept her dad informed of her progress while packing and getting ready. He didn't understand the sudden urgency of her leaving for Alabama but he took it in stride. He didn't ask any questions.

He welcomed her when she arrived at 11 pm. What he didn't know is that she had an incredible journey just getting there.

Cheryl was very much aware of how she survived her own near suicide – without doing anything to cause the police to be called. She simply analyzed it to death.

No pun intended.

OK. Maybe the pun WAS intended.

Her journey to Chicago involved looking wondrously at the sunset as if for the first time while driving through beautiful Wisconsin farmland. The sun was setting in her rear view mirror as the full moon was rising ahead of her, guiding her to Chicago.

It was a reflection of a new chapter in her life. She was leaving her old ways of thinking behind. No more regret. Using the full moon as a guide she was looking at new ways of thinking. She was aware of a God who had always been there for her. She just hadn't been so in touch with it before.

It had been one month since she tried to kill herself. This was a different full moon from July 15.

She never experienced anything like the journey along the same freeway in all her 35 years of travel. She was awake and aware to everything she saw. Yellow flowers along the freeway. Wisconsin farmland with cows and horses and red barns. Gas stations called Love that she stopped at to buy gas and a few souvenirs. The Love gas stations had employees that seemed to really care about people.

She became mesmerized by the moon ahead of her. She drove in quiet most of the time except for listening to some CD's. At one point she turned on a radio station. It was a random station that she picked up somewhere in Wisconsin.

The tune on the radio station was one she recognized. It was the hymn 'Just as I am' also known as 'Lamb of God'. She had grown up playing the piano since she was 8 years old and had learned the words to many hymns throughout the years, including that one.

> *Just as I am, and waiting not*
> *To rid my soul of one dark blot*
> *To Thee whose blood can cleanse each spot*
> *O Lamb of God, I come… I come*

She listened to the song to the end and then turned the radio off.

She drove on in silence. When she became restless, she turned the radio on. This time it was a different station. She was startled to find out the host was talking about suicide attempts. Whoever he was, he not only admitted to trying suicide and having failed at it, but had gotten help over his drug addiction. He was now focused on helping others.

What are the odds?

She asked herself. "What is going on? Am I just more aware of things around me – or is God talking to me through this?"

"I'm driving to Chicago after having this incredible experience over the last several weeks realizing that I have chosen to live rather than die. And I'm listening to a radio in Wisconsin talking about people recovering from suicide attempts. One of the few times I turn on the radio station to experience the world outside my car, someone is talking about suicide."

Hmmmmmm……….

As she arrived late around 11 pm to her father's house in Naperville she realized her journey to Chicago was already very

Spiritual. She couldn't explain it. The moon so incredibly guided her that she couldn't stop thinking about it.

It was magical.

Her dad was glad she arrived safely but he was tired. He was 80 yrs old. Her dad, another guy in her life named Lee, was a wonderful cook. He made a vegetable stew that Cheryl snarfed up. He loved to cook for everybody in his world, not just his family.

"I'm exhausted, Dad. I need to get an early start tomorrow morning if I'm going to make it all the way to Alabama."

She was too tired to explain what had been happening to her over the last several weeks, told him nothing about her near suicide, nor why she was suddenly going to Alabama. He didn't even know she was having problems with Michael.

The only thing she told him was that she was going to a goal-setting church retreat. By herself. Suddenly. Without a lot of planning.

The next morning she was up at 5:30 am. So was her dad. He had drawn one of his special maps outlining the best route from Chicago through Indianapolis and down to Mentone, Alabama.

He was a Planner. He did not go on road trips without a Plan.

He did not understand why she needed to go to Alabama so quickly. He expressed his reservations about her traveling alone.

"I'll be fine, Dad. Don't worry about it. I need to get away from Michael for awhile and this is just the way to do it."

That's all she told him.

Cheryl spent the entire day on the road drinking water and taking far more naps at freeways rest stops than she planned. She was not used to traveling so far by herself. Even when she went to Chicago to visit her Dad, it usually took her a day or two to recover. She didn't have that kind of luxury now.

She was much more tired than she anticipated. She thought she was in shape after all her workouts in the mornings at Bally's with Sheridan, but no matter how physically fit she was the drive took its toll. So did the other tolls along the way.

Pun intended.

By early afternoon she was less than halfway to Alabama. It had been freeway the entire trip but taking longer than she anticipated. She kept calling her dad periodically along the way to update him with her progress. At each call he was concerned that she wasn't as far as she should have been. He was monitoring the trip from his end.

"I guess I'm not a camel like he is. Or most guys for that matter. How can guys travel for hundreds of miles without making pit stops?? Or taking naps?"

It was beyond her... and most women she knew. His estimated time for her arrival in Mentone, Alabama was 5 pm.

At 4 pm she realized there was NO WAY she was going to even come close to the 5 pm target time her dad set for arriving in Mentone. Even the 7 pm opening ceremony of the retreat was not possible. She had been pushing herself to drive as hard and fast as she could, but she was still too far out.

She had to stop and take too many naps. She was exhausted from the drive and her emotional turmoil with Michael. She had not gotten much sleep the day before her trip.

I am really tired. I feel like an Idiot for being so unprepared for this journey. It is taking a lot more out of me than I thought it would. I keep falling asleep while driving... and then I have to stop and take a nap.

Cheryl called the Edwene Gaines' retreat seminar phone number and explained her situation. The receptionist was very friendly and understanding. She told Cheryl that it was more important to just get there.

Alive.

A Saturday morning check-in at the retreat would work for them. At least the retreat center knew she wasn't going to be there Friday night.

Cheryl was relieved. She next called Rebecca, the owner of the bed and breakfast she was staying at called, 'The Inn in the Woods'. Rebecca appreciated the call and said she would not wait up for Cheryl, but would leave a light on in the Ski Room of the bed and breakfast.

Rebecca explained to her that guests stayed in a different building from the main dining area. The guest building was in the woods with cars parked next to it. Each room had a separate entrance.

Rebecca was going to leave the door unlocked to Cheryl's room with the key on the bed. Cheryl was told to look for the room with the light on outside the door of the Ski Room.

That was the key to a series of events that happened later.... Looking for a room with the light on outside the door. Next to a parking lot with cars in it.

Cheryl had directions from Rebecca with her. She felt more relaxed now that she was not under a deadline for the night.

As she drove towards Alabama and the sun was setting behind her, she was again guided by the moon in front of her. All she had to do was follow the moon which was low in the sky. Guiding her as a big bright light just above the horizon.

She drove deeper and deeper into the night. She listened to a few more of her CD's as well as the silence until she became aware of a strange sound coming from the trees as she raced along the dark freeway with the windows open.

The sound resembled an exotic bird.

What kind of birds do they have down here in this part of the country that sound like that? What do they look like? They must be huge to be making such a noise!! There have to be hundreds of them.

She was so fascinated by the bird calls in the trees that she stopped the car to listen to them. It was close to 10 pm. With all her pit stops it had gotten to be that late.

The scene she saw will remain in her mind forever. It was the Chattanooga Valley in Tennessee with the moon outlining the dark hills. No lights were in the hills. The moon was so bright that she could see all the edges of the hills. The sky was clear with a million stars. She felt as if she was on another planet.

She was mesmerized by the birds. The calls were loud and incredible. She stopped for several minutes along the freeway and noticed no cars were coming in either direction. She got out of the car to really listen. She was alone on a freeway at night with only the moon and the birds.

It took her breath away.

She thanked God for such an incredibly beautiful experience.

Another revelation. She wouldn't have had the experience if she were dead.

After several minutes of enjoying the peacefulness and serenity of the situation she carefully got back in her car. Before starting the car she turned on the radio. She had no idea what station it was.

What she heard was the beginning of an amazing instrumental version of the hymn, 'Lamb of God'. Also known as 'Just as I Am'. Even though it was an instrumental version with no words, she knew the words by heart.

> *Just as I am, and waiting not*
> *To rid my soul of one dark blot,*
> *To Thee whose blood can cleanse each spot,*
>   *O Lamb of God, I come... I come.*

Oh My God. Not again!

It was the *same song* as the previous night on the radio while driving to Chicago. The only other hymn she had heard on the radio. Most of the time she drove in silence.

This particular arrangement included nearly every instrument she'd ever heard. Saxophones, clarinets, violins and French horns. Cheryl learned how to play the saxophone in her Irondale High School band of New Brighton so knew how to pick out different musical instruments in a song.

Saxophones were easy for her to learn after playing the piano. It was only one note at a time. How hard could that be?

She held her breath and did not drive away. She stayed, stopped, along the freeway during the entire song. The song, combined with the birds, put her into a different world.

No cars drove by the freeway during the entire song. She was completely alone.

She felt like she was the only one on the planet.

At the end of the song, a low Grand Canyon sexy-sounding announcer came on the radio. His voice was deep. He said, "Well folks, that was the first time we've ever played that song on this station. In fact, I've never even heard it before. It's called 'Lamb of God' by ....."

Oh My God! OMG.

What is going on here? Where am I going? What is in Alabama that I need to see? What is this journey I'm on to Mentone, Alabama?

What is this Lamb of God thing happening? Just as I am, I come… I come.

The announcer mentioned the arranger of the song but Cheryl didn't recognize the name. And she forgot to write it down. Or the radio station. All she remembered was his deep sounding words. It

TREA$URE YOUR LIFE | 117

was the first time either one of them had heard it on the air. Or anybody who was listening that night.

Cheryl held her breath as she turned the keys to start the car. What if it didn't start on this deserted freeway?

But it did. Her Toyota Corolla Sport always started right up.

Now she had to continue on her journey.

A short time later she realized she had to make another pit stop so she stopped at the next freeway Rest Stop. It was getting close to 11 pm. It was a fairly elaborate rest stop. Not typical of the other ones she'd seen.

This rest stop had what looked like a ranger station nestled in the trees. It was lit up enough at night so the entire place felt safe. She got out of the car and walked around. The signs described in detail about DeSoto discovering the area and how there was a park named after this Spanish guy. A waterfall was even named after him. The DeSoto Falls.

Cheryl had never heard of him. What she didn't know is that DeSoto Falls was going to be mentioned over and over to her in the part of Alabama she was headed for. It was the main attraction for the area around Mentone.

She was heading directly into it.

Before getting back in her car, she stopped a guy walking his little white dog in the parking lot of the freeway rest stop.

She asked him if he was from around there.

"Yes, Ma'am."

"Could you tell me what kind of birds those are in the trees making all that noise?"

"Birds? Those aren't birds, Ma'am. Those are Tree Frogs."

"What?!! You mean you have *frogs* up in *trees* down here?!!" She thought he was kidding.

"Yes, Ma'am. We do."

What the ?!!!! He looked at her as if she was crazy for not knowing that and she looked at him as if he was crazy for telling her that.

She couldn't believe it. Tree Frogs??

Back in Minnesota frogs didn't climb up in trees. They stayed in ponds. And they didn't make noises like exotic birds. How could frogs sound like birds??? Weren't they supposed to croak?!

Where in the world am I? She thought she was losing her mind.

Am I still on the same planet as when I left yesterday??

She began to wonder...

Chapter 6 ~ Setting a Goal

Cheryl drove on in silence in the darkness towards Alabama. She listened to the tree frogs up in the trees, still not believing what the guy at the DeSoto Falls rest stop had told her.

"I wonder if he was on drugs? He didn't seem like it though. He did talk funny ~ that Southern accent. And calling me Ma'am. I'm not used to that. He was so polite."

She contemplated all that had happened since July 15. How alive she felt. How unexpected Life was!

In the silence of her car, she thought about the U2 band concert she had gone to since July 15. It was a spur of the moment decision on a Saturday evening in early August that prompted her to attend the concert. She talked Michael into riding their bicycles the few blocks to the U of M Gopher stadium so they could watch the concert from the horseshoe entrance.

It was one of the best concerts she had seen in her life. And it was FREE for them! They were watching the huge screens that could be seen from outside the stadium. Michael lasted for only a few songs. It was too loud for him and he became restless. He said he had to go back home to work on a client's website.

Cheryl thought, "Oh well. At least I got him out for some fun."

She wondered if he would have stayed longer if he had been with Angie.

Cheryl stayed for the entire concert, including the intense rainstorm towards the end of the concert.

U2 played in the downpour and lightening storm in Minneapolis. It felt great on that hot summer night!

She talked to other bicyclists after Michael left. She met a guy named Steve. He was married but his wife was not there with him. Steve was someone who rode his bicycle home with her later that night in the intense rainstorm to make sure she got there OK.

She looked for her friend, Sheridan who told her he might show up with Katherine, but she couldn't find him. Cheryl didn't want to leave her spot next to her bicycle. And it was too difficult to navigate through the crowd with her bicycle. Hundreds of people were outside the stadium watching the U2 concert on the big screens. The concert was sold-out inside.

She found out later that Sheridan was there with Katherine only about 100 feet from where she was, but she never saw either one of them.

She didn't know much about the U2 band but the commotion surrounding the 1-½ week setup was something that her neighborhood could not possibly ignore. It was practically in Prospect Park's backyard.

The U2 concert was all over the Twin Cities (← Minneapolis and St. Paul) news. The concert took over a week to set up because the stage was so elaborate. There were about 100 silver and red semi-trailers parked around the Gopher stadium for a week.

She remembered as she was driving to Alabama that she spent the entire Saturday of the U2 concert attending a Communication Seminar that Michael insisted they go to together.

Alone and in the silence of her car she finally had time to think about all the events since July 15. When she had decided to Live. Including the Communication Seminar on the day of the U2 concert only a few weeks *after* July 15.

She remembered her brother, Jerry, calling during the morning of the seminar to ask if he could park his car in their driveway in Prospect Park and walk to the U2 concert. Jerry was going with his wife Barb, and their pastor Peter and his wife. Jerry assumed parking around the Gopher Stadium was going to be a nightmare.

A Lutheran pastor going to a U2 concert? "He must be pretty cool," said Cheryl to herself.

Cheryl thought of these things as she was driving towards Mentone, Alabama.

The Communication Seminar changed her perspective on her marriage. It had given her new insight into why she and Michael had many misunderstandings.

What started out as a seminar on coping with Communication issues between people of different races gradually evolved that Saturday into two separate groups: a Poor vs Rich view of the world.

The seminar leaders divided and separated the participants into 2 different groups based on whether they grew up Rich or Poor according to each participant's individual analysis. Michael and Cheryl were in opposite groups – based on how they viewed themselves growing up. The leaders had specific questions to use as a guide.

Cheryl *never* thought of herself as having grown up Rich. She only realized that she had *not* grown up Poor. At least according to the questions they all had to answer.

Cheryl walked back into the seminar after a break where she called her brother Jerry back and worked out the parking arrangements for that night's U2 concert. She noticed the class size had gotten much smaller. One of the leaders was writing stuff on a white board. She sat on a chair next to Michael.

He turned to her and whispered, "Uh, Cheryl. You're in the wrong group."

"What?"

She was embarrassed at being in the wrong place. Michael quietly explained that right after the break the class was separated into two groups: Rich and Poor. Cheryl belonged in the conference room with the Rich people. It had been explained to the class while she was on the phone talking to her brother.

Cheryl apologized and went into the conference room where the Rich people were talking about how they viewed Poor people as they were growing up. It was unbelievable to her what these people were saying. They were really getting into the role-acting part of being Rich.

They were saying things about the Poor like, "They are lazy. They are too dumb to get a job. They don't want to try. They don't care about what they are doing. They get angry all the time. Their houses are a mess."

She was shocked and appalled! How could they really think that?

Knowing it was an exercise in group dynamics, she mostly kept silent. It was character play-acting in a group setting. She knew they were exaggerating their perceptions.

The Rich group found out later when they were all combined into the large group that the Poor group's response to the Rich group were things like, "They think we are dumb. They think we are lazy. They constantly criticize us no matter what we do. They don't listen to us."

They think we are worthless.

The two groups had an equal number of participants. This meant that whoever signed up for the seminar didn't know whether they had grown up Rich or Poor. They were just interested in learning more about coping with Communication issues.

In Cheryl's mind it completely changed her view of their marriage. She came to a new understanding of why her husband so hated the Rich. She was in one group and Michael was in the other. She had been born into one, and he into the other. She was not really Rich, but she had not grown up Poor either.

It explained why he was always criticizing her Dad, her brothers and anybody else who had money. Cheryl tried to be sympathetic to him. She could not understand why he didn't want to go to Marco Island to her dad's condo, or why he didn't want to go to her brother Jerry's house in Wayzata for bar-b-q's. Or her brother Terry's house in Lakeville for holiday dinners.

Both her brothers were doing well and had beautiful houses. As did her Dad. All of their houses were clean and organized. There was no clutter. No piles of newspapers were laying around in any of their houses.

Michael didn't want to associate with anybody who had money …
for any reason *except* political (Democratic) fund-raising.

Michael had grown up Poor and felt intimidated by the Rich. He was taught to hate them by his parents. He despised the Rich no matter who they were…. In his eyes he thought THEY considered him a low-life.

And worthless.

Which he was *not*.

These insights to Cheryl came to her as she was driving to Alabama.

She finally had time to think.

She realized that she and Michael were really quite different. So different that her husband used Anger to deal with things he couldn't control.

It was how he was raised.

Even though Michael's father did not use drugs or alcohol, Michael's father used Rage as his drug. Michael's grandfather also used the same Rage drug. It was generational.

After Michael's close friend Dan invited both of them to a Grief Ritual a week after Cheryl's father's 80th birthday celebration, Michael made an effort to contact the long-lost relatives of his Father's side of the family.

Michael would go off on a Rage tirade as if he was possessed by a Demon. Cheryl witnessed that many times over the course of their marriage. Michael found out by contacting his cousins that it was exactly what his Grandfather did. And his Uncle.

All their Rage episodes happened as quickly as if they were striking a match. With no warning. As if possessed by some Walt Disney cartoon demon. Walt Disney was good at making demons appear instantly and look really scary.

During the Communications Seminar, Cheryl heard that this behavior was typical of those who considered themselves Poor. Not everybody, but a large majority of them were like Michael. They had hatred for those who had money. They took out their hatred by getting angry. They used their anger to try and control those around them. Their Anger appeared quickly!

Some of them felt cheated by their upbringing and tried to take it out on those closest to them. Cheryl not only heard thoughts from Michael about this but from others in the group at the seminar.

It was a new awakening for her. Michael's behavior was not unique.

She felt helpless. She gained a new understanding in what it must have been like growing up Poor.

As she was driving to Alabama she realized how different she was from Michael. Cheryl had *not* grown up Rich but she had grown up in a loving middle-class family. Cheryl's dad was smart and invested his money wisely. Her dad was now doing very well for someone who started out as a truck driver for Land O' Lakes.

Cheryl was not afraid of her Dad. He never hit her or yelled at her or abused her. Michael's father had physically abused Michael several times while he was growing up. Michael's father routinely hit him and yelled at him and abused him. His father also did that to Michael's mother.

She wondered as she drove to Alabama if she and Michael were going to make it this time. His Rage was really destroying their relationship. She could see now that he couldn't help it. Just as *she* had grown up loving people, *he* had grown up abusing those closest to him because that's all he knew.

It was starting to make sense to her now that she had time to think. So many things had been happening to her since July 15 that she hadn't processed it all.

For the first time in her marriage, she started looking at the possibility of ending it.

How could she do it, though? She had no job. No real money saved up, except some stocks. No place to live.

Well, she'd have to give it more serious thought. This was her 2nd marriage, after all. Both times she got married with the intention of it lasting her lifetime. The thought of failing again at a marriage was not something she looked forward to.

She really loved Michael and intended to be with him for the rest of her life. That's what her wedding vows to him said.

She didn't see the Rage within him until their 1st anniversary. They were vacationing in Sydney, Australia. It was a day she would never forget. He started an argument with her that afternoon in Sydney that prevented them from having a wonderful romantic dinner that night.

His anger turned into outright Rage. She remembered it had something to do with deciding what restaurant they were going to eat at that night. How could that have been such a problem?

Intuitively Cheryl decided she did not want to have children with him even though they had talked about it. Because he became so incredibly angry over *nothing* she suddenly changed her mind. She wasn't used to that. She was 37 years old and capable of getting pregnant. She saw his Rage turn him into a demon almost instantly.

After his Rage took over in Australia, she didn't talk to him for the next 24 hours.

He knew he had really blown it. He kept trying to make it up to her. What they both didn't realize at the time was that he had also blown the one chance they had to have children. He didn't have any children and wanted at least one.

She pondered these things as she drove along to Alabama. She remembered that Michael made her sign a prenuptial the day before they got married that said in the case of divorce, the house was his. She had no problem signing a prenuptial agreement because she never intended to get divorced from him.

Suddenly everything was different.

She felt stronger and more confident than she had since her layoff from the University. Her relationship with Michael had changed dramatically since she'd lost the ability to bring in money. She used to be the main breadwinner, making more money than he did. She also carried the medical and insurance benefits.

What could she offer him these days? Nothing. Except a clean house and someone who cooked for him.

Was that the Purpose of her Life?

As she drove closer to Alabama and pondered these things she decided that maybe she could make a difference in other people's lives if she wrote a book. About how she decided NOT to end her own life.

If it would prevent people from committing suicide and doing something they might regret as a Spirit, it might allow them to Trea$ure their Life.

Yes, she had learned how to Trea$ure her Life. Especially after coming so close to ending it.

She knew that going to the goal setting retreat in Alabama was for setting goals. She read the description and talked to the seminar folks before signing up. It was explained to her that those who attended this particular seminar should have some goals in mind they wanted to focus on.

She had NO goals when she set out on her journey to Alabama. The only goal she had was to get away from Michael for awhile.

"That's it then. My goal will be to write a book. I've never done that before. English was my *worst* subject in school. I hated it. I *especially* hated writing anything. But Now is the Time to think outside of myself. I need to stretch and tackle something I've never done before. I feel so much alive."

I could be dead.

The book will be called *"Trea$ure Your Life"* with a dollar sign in the title.

Chapter 7 ~ Finding Mentone

Cheryl finally arrived close to Mentone in the Northeast corner of Alabama around midnight. She could tell it was a remote mountain location, nestled in the hills. Because she was extremely tired by that time, she got confused and turned around by the directions she was given.

She found herself following the Moon and getting lost.

She panicked for a bit and stopped at a gas station that was still open to ask for directions to her bed and breakfast. The Inn in the Woods. A customer in the gas station offered to drive ahead and lead her close to where she was supposed to go.

"These people in Alabama are sure nice," Cheryl thought. "It's almost Midnight."

As she followed the woman in the SUV ahead of her she noticed a train racing along next to the road. The two cars were traveling at the same pace as the train. The train let out the whistle that trains do. With her windows open she heard the train call to her. The moon was guiding them all.

'It's all right.' The whistle seemed to be saying. 'Just follow her.'

The train was going to be her guide in the future. She didn't know that.

At a fork in the road, the woman ahead of her motioned with her arm out the window for Cheryl to go ahead.

They had agreed that the woman was going to lead her to a point where Cheryl should be able to figure out the rest of the way. At least she was entering Mentone, Alabama.

Cheryl drove up the mountain to a four-way stop. She looked to the right and saw The Mentone Inn. Wonderful! She had arrived.

Or so she thought.

She remembered Rebecca telling her that the light would be on outside the room she was supposed to be in and that cars would be in a parking lot right next to it.

Cheryl saw the cars in the parking lot. She turned to the right and pulled into the parking lot. Then got out of her car. She noticed a light on in a separate building outside a door. This matched the description she was given from Rebecca. She walked towards the light. The door was locked.

How could this be? It was the only light on in a separate building next to a parking lot with cars. She walked around the building looking for other lights. She found none. Cheryl went back to the first place where she saw the light on outside a door.

She tried the door again. It was still locked.

Of course.

She was in Mentone. She knew that much. She had seen the sign. The town was only 2 blocks long. She was extremely tired but she walked around the building again. She felt deflated.

What was wrong? She was so close and yet so far away. She did not have a room.

After walking around the building a 3rd time and really noticing everything about it she realized it was a CHURCH!

"What the ----?!!!'"

She was trying to find the unlocked door to a bed and breakfast with a light on and she was actually dealing with an Episcopal church next to a place called The Mentone Inn. Suddenly she remembered that The Mentone Inn was *not* the right place!! She had been too tired to realize she was supposed to be at a place called the Inn in the Woods.

Her Project Manager mind had to pay attention to details and this one escaped her when she parked her car ~ due to her exhausted state of mind.

She noticed a sign that said St Joseph's on the Mountain Episcopal Church.

Oh NO!! Where in the world was she? Where was the bed and breakfast called the Inn in the Woods?

She almost gave up and spent the night in her car, she was so tired.

But then she heard music. Across the street. At Midnight.

It was magical.

"What the ---??!!" She was in the middle of a small town that was two blocks long in northern Alabama on a Friday night. Who could possibly be up at that hour?

She needed to talk to someone to find out what to do. There were no gas stations open. In fact, she did not see any gas stations at all from the top of the mountain in Mentone. She heard laughter and voices and Real People.

She walked across the street to another inn called The Mentone Springs Hotel. The Hotel looked like it was about a hundred years old with an old-fashioned white porch and lots of windows. It was absolutely beautiful. She felt like she was in a movie.

It was surreal. Or was she just so tired that she was dreaming it?

"This is amazing!"

As she approached the hotel she saw 20 people laughing and partying. They were dressed very well as if they were at an elaborate function. They were sitting at a long table with a white tablecloth and candles on the table. It looked as if a fancy dinner had been served. The lights were soft and low.

It was a warm summer night. All the doors were open to the outside so anyone could walk in. She entered into a scene that she would never forget.

She saw an attractive woman who looked like Marie Osmond playing the piano as 4 guys were leaning on the piano singing in perfect harmony. One of the guys played the guitar. All the guys looked alike. They were laughing and smiling as they sang, completely at ease performing for the small crowd.

They had that good-looking movie star quality one sees in late night movies.

She identified with the woman playing the piano. The one who looked like Marie Osmond. Except Cheryl didn't think of herself as that cute. But she knew what it was like to play the piano with people singing around her.

Cheryl remembered how her dad and his brother Larry performed at many weddings, family reunions and parties. Larry played the guitar and had a close friend named Marv who played the accordian with them. Cheryl had grown up hearing them practice often.

Her grandfather's four sisters were known as The Lindberg Sisters. They had a successful singing reputation in their local town of Scandia, Minnesota. They sounded very much like The Andrews Sisters who were also from Minnesota.

What Cheryl walked into was a family situation she had experienced growing up. She remembered family gatherings of talented musical people. She tried to be subtle as she slipped into the room. She was drawn to a woman in a dark blue dress. The deep blue represented her mother's Spirit.

"Hi", she said to the woman in the blue dress. "I'm lost. I'm from Minnesota and I'm trying to find the Inn in the Woods. Do you know where that is?"

The woman in the blue dress didn't know where it was. She explained to Cheryl that this was a rehearsal dinner for a wedding the next day at The Mentone Springs Hotel. The people at the piano were practicing for their performance.

It was 4 brothers and their sister who had grown up singing together. Similar to the Osmond family. One of the brothers had a daughter getting married the next day. They were all staying at the Inn.

The song they were practicing was the Everly Brothers' song *'Devoted to You'*. It was incredible.

Darling you can count on me
Till the sun dries up the sea
Until then I'll always be
Devoted . . .   to you

Through the years my love will grow
Like a river it will flow
It can't die because I'm so
Devoted . . .   to you

Beautiful and magical.

They sang together as if they had one voice ~ but different harmonizing notes. Their voices blended together perfectly.

"Who in the world are they?" She wondered. But did not ask.

She found out they lived in different parts of the country. They grew up in the part of Alabama near Mentone, which was why the wedding was taking place at The Mentone Springs Hotel. It was a rare and special event for them all to be together.

The woman in the blue dress offered Cheryl some champagne, which Cheryl gladly took to relax. Cheryl was captivated listening to the beautiful music the group was making. She didn't want to leave. If she could have slept underneath the table that night she would have.

But that would *not* have been appropriate.

Cheryl finally asked the woman in the blue dress to help her find someone of The Mentone Springs Hotel who knew how to find directions to the Inn in the Woods.

A young woman working at the hotel knew exactly where Cheryl needed to go. She knew Rebecca from the Inn in the Woods. She said, "It's only another 15 minutes away."

"What???!!!" Cheryl was exhausted. How could this be? After all this travel she was finally in Mentone and it was still another 15 minutes away? She figured it was right around the corner someplace. The town was only two blocks long after all.

At least she had more specific directions. Go down the road, turn this way on the first dirt road, take a left on another dirt road --- etc. Follow the directions exactly and you'll get there.

What Cheryl didn't know at the time was that The Mentone Springs Hotel was going to be a major turning point in her life a few days later. As was the St. Joseph's on the Mountain Episcopal Church across the street.

If she had stopped at the stop sign at the top of the mountain and gone right past these two places with the directions the first time, her life might have been very different.

Cheryl thanked the nice young lady, said goodbye to the family wedding group and took the piece of paper with the directions. She followed the directions exactly. She was a Project Manager after all and knew how to deal with information.

She arrived at the Inn in the Woods according to the directions she now had. It was almost 1 am. She was truly exhausted but exhilarated at the same time.

She saw the cars parked in the parking lot as Rebecca had explained. She found the separate building with a light on outside a room. She looked inside the windows first to make sure. It was the Ski Room. She saw old-fashioned snow skis on the wall.

This was not a church.

She made it!

She laughed as she entered the unlocked room with a note on the bed that said: 'Welcome, Cheryl. Here's your key.'

She looked more closely at the antique snow skis on the wall (she was from Minnesota after all) and other things like a small moose on a table. The proprietor explained to her over the phone when she made the reservation that this area was the only area in Alabama that offered skiing. It was in the mountains.

The Ski Room was the only room left for the weekend. And it was the first place she had contacted for the retreat.

Then Cheryl entered the bathroom.

And said out loud, *"Oh My God! OMG!"*

The bathroom wallpaper consisted of books on shelves. Completely covering the bathroom. The shower, over the sink, over the towels. Everything.

Who in their right mind would decorate a bathroom with wallpaper covered in books??!

Was this a joke? Was God talking to her again??

With so many stops she had to make on the trip down spending time in bathrooms, this was too much. She laughed hysterically.

OK. I got it. Thank you God.

Now I'm going to bed.

Chapter 8 ~ The Donkey

Cheryl woke up at 5 am the next morning and immediately started laughing.

"A bathroom covered in books??? Come on, God. Are you trying to get my attention? Do you do this to everybody who checks into this room? Do they all write books?"

"Or do they just read them in the bathroom?"

It was too Funny.

She was exhausted from her long drive the previous day but woke up at 5 am anyway. It was her usual wake up time.

She stretched out on the bed and looked outside the window. The screen on the open window let the smell of the warm summer air into the room. The night before she didn't care what it looked like outside her room because she barely crawled into bed. She was ready to spend the night in her car.

It was a new day. She made it to ALABAMA!!! Wow. Over 1,000 miles driving on her own in 2 days. Farther than she had ever driven by herself. With nobody beside her to help with the drive. And she didn't fall asleep and kill anybody.

Her thoughts were racing.

It doesn't matter what this Goal Setting retreat is going to be about. The journey here has been so spiritual and magical that I've

ALREADY gotten my money's worth for the retreat I've paid for in advance.

I am noticing God everywhere in my life right now.

Life is worth paying attention to.

I think all people on this planet have the opportunity in their lives to notice signs from God. Most of the time, they just don't notice these things. They are simply not paying attention.

She remembered the incredible experience the night before in the Chattanooga Valley. The moon outlining the dark hills while she was driving. How incredibly marvelous it was to stop along the freeway (a FREEWAY of all things) and have everything around her be quiet except for the Tree Frogs. No cars coming in either direction for several minutes.

Ah yes, the Tree Frogs. Frogs up in trees? Making sounds like exotic birds? What kind of a place was this? Are they nuts??!

She remembered turning on the radio as the instrumental version of 'Lamb of God' was just starting. It was truly a spiritual moment for her that she would never forget. Not only was the arrangement of the song incredibly beautiful, the Lamb of God song was the same song she heard the night before on the radio as she was going to Chicago.

It was one of the few times she even turned on the radio. Most of the time she drove in silence.

She remembered the talk of suicide by the announcer on one of the other few times she turned on the radio as she was driving through Wisconsin on Thursday night. How he had faced it and worked through his own attempt. How he was trying to help others.

What did it all mean?

If she could have been transported back home to Minnesota at that moment like they did on Star Trek, it all would have been worth it.

She felt on Saturday morning her journey was complete.

What she saw in the early morning light outside her window at the Inn in the Woods bed and breakfast were trees that seemed endless. She stopped breathing for a moment as she heard footsteps outside her window. It was the sound of steps on the dry crackling leaves coming closer and closer.

Oh no!! Who was sneaking up on her? At this hour?? It was 5 am!!

As she lay there motionless but with her eyes open... like a Dragonfly ... she waited. And then she saw who was making the footsteps.

It was a single deer. About 10 feet away from her. She could see the lashes of its eyes.

A beautiful graceful deer. The deer stopped moving and looked through the window at her. She couldn't believe it.

I really am in the middle of nowhere in the woods, aren't I? There's a deer right outside my window!! Only 10 feet away.

Oh My God! OMG!

She had never experienced anything like it. She felt safe and protected from her lookout place. The deer stopped and stared at her for a few moments.

She held her breath. Then she heard other footsteps and noticed a 2nd deer alongside the first one. They both stopped and looked at her. She still wasn't breathing. She didn't want to scare them off so she didn't dare move to get her camera.

She simply enjoyed the moment.

She remembered somebody told her once if a deer looks at you for a long time, it is because they are Spiritual. And you are lucky when they do that.

Whatever. Who really knows?

After what seemed like an Eternity, both deer quietly walked off into the woods. Cheryl was too excited to go back to sleep. She got up and decided to explore the area outside.

She went outside and heard a falls or rapids or some kind of running water off in the distance. She started walking towards the sound. It took her awhile and she never quite saw the water but she at least was able to assess the situation.

She was on a mountaintop next to a river valley that dropped down several hundred feet. It was so high that she could not see the river below but could hear the water running. It was a beautiful scene. Very peaceful and relaxing. She realized that she had made the right choice and had gotten lucky finding such an enchanting bed and breakfast.

What she realized much later was that the falls she heard was the DeSoto Falls. She never saw the falls.

The proprietor of the bed and breakfast, Rebecca, told her the night before while she was traveling that breakfast was served every morning at 8 am. Promptly. She was advised not to be late.

Cheryl walked around the early morning and explored the grounds. She figured out where the main building was that probably served breakfast.

She loved the woodsy smell of the beautiful forest grounds. After walking around and exploring for 2 hours she went back to her room to get ready for breakfast.

She had identified the correct building for breakfast and arrived before 8 am. She felt confident again after her previous night of going to the wrong place (an Episcopal church in Mentone) thinking it was a bed and breakfast. She felt stupid for making such a mistake. She decided to share that experience with the other guests to explain why she showed up so late.

After sharing her story with the guests, they all laughed and welcomed her. Even Rebecca laughed.

Cheryl had a spirited conversation with the other 7 guests who were a combination of couples and single people. She found out two of the women staying there were also attending the Edwene Gaines' Goal Setting retreat.

She had a wonderful breakfast of homemade egg soufflé. Rebecca made Cheryl a special side serving that was gluten-free, which was exquisite. Rebecca was experimenting with gluten-free recipes because she had been getting more requests for them. Rebecca was happy to accommodate the special request.

Cheryl had been diagnosed as gluten-intolerant two years before and found it challenging to find foods that she could eat without wheat. She had to eliminate flour, pasta, crackers, many processed foods, oatmeal, cereal and bread from her diet. It was difficult.
As a conversation item, Cheryl couldn't help but ask what some of the other guests had as bathroom wallpaper.

"Huh?" They asked.

"You know," said Cheryl. "What wallpaper is in your bathroom? Mine has books."

"Oh" – one of them said. "Mine has bunnies." Another one had deer. A third one had butterflies. Nobody else had books.

"Just wondering." Said Cheryl nonchalantly. She didn't explain why.

She connected with the women from the Edwene Gaines' retreat who were from different parts of the country. Anna was from New Jersey, Sandy was from California. Both had flown into a nearby city Friday morning and driven rental cars through the country to Mentone.

After the wonderful breakfast, both women told Cheryl that they were not to be late for the Saturday morning check-in. Edwene made a point of telling everyone the night before at the Friday opening ceremony that she wanted people to be on time. Promptly by 9:30 am.

Cheryl figured out that Edwene was one of those who wanted people to make sure they were not late.

Anna was a high-spirited woman who offered to drive ahead of Cheryl and show her where the retreat center was. It was located in Valley Head about 20 minutes away.

What Cheryl discovered is that Anna from New Jersey drove down the mountain like a crazy person, just like the racing legend Mario Andretti. How could she drive so fast around those curves of the mountain? It was exhilarating!

"I survived my own suicide attempt but I might not survive this!" Cheryl laughed to herself.

Sandy was following Cheryl and right on her tail. They were all racing down the curves of the mountain. All 3 of them together. Tight. As a Team.

After arriving frantically to the retreat center the 2 *other* women took off running.

"Hurry up! We'll be late!!" They shouted to her.

They all ran to one building, threw their purses down and then ran to a smaller building.

The smaller building was a meditation room with the most incredible smell of incense Cheryl had ever experienced. The three women who raced down the mountain together were not the last to arrive. A few others arrived after them. Cheryl was glad they were not late although it seemed that things had already started.

After a brief introduction to the music and meditation by Edwene, Cheryl settled in to the peacefulness of the scene. She felt like she was in another world. She didn't have any concept of Time. It didn't seem to matter.

She had only met Edwene 2 weeks before when Edwene spoke at her Unity Christ Church in Golden Valley. Cheryl thought Edwene had a great sense of Humor. One thing she looked for in people was a sense of Humor.

Cheryl created this phrase and used it often: 'Smart people tend to be Funny and Funny people tend to be Smart.'

Edwene was definitely Funny which in Cheryl's eyes made her Smart. Cheryl hadn't laughed that much at a sermon in a long time. Both Edwene (an ordained Unity minister) and the pastor of Cheryl's church, Reverend Pat Williamson, were from Alabama. They were good friends within the Unity church community. They both raved about the beauty of Alabama to those in Minnesota.

After her recent experiences in Alabama, Cheryl had to agree. It was a beautiful place.

Following the meditation, Edwene invited Cheryl to the front of the meditation room to introduce herself. During the Friday night ceremony everybody had the opportunity to introduce themselves and explain why they were attending the retreat. Cheryl missed the chance to hear others, but Edwene explained that she would get to know them over the course of the weekend.

For now, Edwene wanted Cheryl to explain a bit about herself and what her goal was.

Cheryl briefly outlined what she had been through since July 15 when she wanted to end her life, and that she wanted to write about it to help others. That was pretty much it.

After Cheryl's introduction, Edwene told everybody they would take a break and walk back to the main retreat building.

The group spent the rest of the day working on clarifying their goals.

In the middle of the afternoon, Edwene gave everybody a loonnng break. Enough to leave the retreat center if they wanted to. They all had to be back at a specific time.

Cheryl decided to head for Mentone again.

She took off in her silver Toyota Corolla Sport vehicle and headed back to the mountain. She got as far as the top of the mountain and looked around this time in the daylight. It was a cute town. Only 2 blocks long but with some character.

Cheryl discovered a restaurant called The Wildflower Café that looked interesting. She parked her car and walked in. It was cozy and inviting. She noticed they had outside seating. She always sat outside a restaurant whenever possible. Minnesota winters were so cold that it was a treat to sit outside in the warm summer air.

So despite the option of air conditioning, she chose on a hot summer day to sit outside. The restaurant inside had lots of people.

She was alone outside. In the sun.

Or so she thought.

She brought retreat materials with her to continue writing and answering questions that Edwene provided for the group to do. After awhile, she noticed she was not alone.

An older guy was sitting off to one side under a tent in the shade. She saw he had a guitar. How cool is that? Cheryl was always interested in meeting other musicians.

She looked up and made eye contact with him. He smiled, and said, "Hi. You're not from around here are you?"

She figured everybody in this small town knew everybody so she probably stood out. Plus who in their right mind would want to sit outside on a hot 90 degree day? In the sun?

"Nope. I'm from Minneapolis. I just got in last night. I'm attending an Edwene Gaines retreat. Have you heard of her?"

"Of course," he replied. "Everybody around here knows who she is. She's very well known in these parts. So, if you're from Minneapolis do you know Robert Bly?" He asked.

"What??!!" She exclaimed. "Of course I do. Actually, my husband Michael knows him really well. I've only met Robert Bly once. He used to live two houses away from my husband in Prospect Park."

"Well, imagine that." He explained that he knew Robert Bly very well, too. Robert Bly was the author of *'Iron Man'*. And many other men's books. He had a national reputation for being a leader of men's issues.

"So how in the world do you know Robert? Does he come here?" She asked.

"Yup. He comes here to this area for men's retreats. He has a good friend in these parts named John and they organize seminars together. Or at least they used to. Until Robert's health started affecting him."

"Yeah," said Cheryl. "I've heard that from Michael, too. Robert is starting to become weaker and not doing as much anymore."

"So, what's your name?" She asked him.

"Tony. I play the guitar here at this place. Edwene knows me very well."

"Well, my name is Cher," she told him.

She realized at that moment it was odd for her to say that to a complete stranger. It was NOT odd for her to introduce herself, but it was odd for her to use THAT name: *Cher.*

Her real name was Cheryl. She had decided for church events she would be known as Cher. She was at a church retreat and had registered as Cher, so it seemed appropriate she tell Tony that.

After all, she was wearing a nametag that clearly said Cher.

Cheryl went on to explain to Tony that her nickname was Cher and that she had been called Cher since she was a teenager long before there was *another* famous Cher. She also told him that her nickname was Sunny because she loved the sun so much. That's why she was sitting in the sun on a hot summer day, when there was air conditioning inside.

"So I'm really Sunny AND Cher."

Tony laughed.

"Well, I'll remember that one," he said. "That's pretty good."

Cheryl talked to him for a bit longer before going back to her writing.

How odd was it that in this small town she was still connected to someone back in Minneapolis? Robert Bly of all people. Someone Michael knew personally.

She thought of Michael again. She wondered what he was doing back home. She decided to call him from her cell phone. She hadn't talked to him since she left Minnesota.

"Hi, Dear," she asked him. "How are you doing?"

He was working as usual. He sounded happy to hear from her at first. She told him of the retreat, how she had arrived very late the night before and that it was going very well. She had also arrived

TREA$URE YOUR LIFE | 149

late at her dad's house the night before that. It was the first chance she had to tell him anything.

Some might have thought it odd that it took her 2 days to call Michael from her cell phone after she left Minneapolis. But Michael was not an early morning riser as she was, so she did not want to bother him when she woke up that morning at 5 am. She had gotten in too late the night before so didn't want to call him then, either.

Her friend Sally had been conditioning Cheryl to not talk on her cell phone while driving. It was illegal to do that in California and Sally warned her it would become more common not to talk on cell phones and drive at the same time in other states, too. That was why she hadn't talked to her husband at all since she left.

It was her conversation with Tony that prompted her to call Michael.

She told Michael what had just happened. Michael knew the guy named John that Tony mentioned who was Robert Bly's friend from northern Alabama. Michael said, "I think I have a picture of me with this guy named John. It was taken at a men's retreat in Minneapolis that we organized with Robert Bly."

Amazing how small the world is. Her husband was in a picture with a guy who knew someone she just met. Michael also had a reputation for being a leader of men's issues.

They talked about normal stuff married people talk about. Then Michael got another phone call. It was from a client. They had to cut the conversation short.

Typical. She thought.

Oh well, she needed to get away from him for awhile so this was probably the best. At least they weren't getting into another argument over Angie. Or his newspapers. Or Cheryl being in Alabama without a job.

Cheryl headed back to the Valley Head retreat center after enjoying the sunshine (Sunny was her nickname after all) and a wonderful lunch.

On the way back she was driving very slowly along the last dirt road before heading up the hill when she heard the most awful sound! It sounded like someone crying out in trouble.

She stopped the car and looked around. Then she heard it again. And again.

What in the world was that noise? It sounded dreadful.

She got out of her car to try and figure out what it was. She was parked along a dirt road between two pastures. On one side she saw a donkey. Then it called out to her.

BRAHH UHH! BRAHHHHHHH UHH!

Oh My God! OMG.

The donkey seemed to be calling to her. What in the world? She went over to it. The donkey came right up to the white rail fence. She had never been close to a donkey before in her life. A horse, yes, but not a donkey.

She had a small bag of carrots with her as a snack. Ever since her fire cleaning episode with Sheridan 2 years before she often had carrots with her. She gave the donkey a carrot. He sniffed it and then took the small carrot immediately. He seemed to love it. So she gave him another one. And another one. He ate almost the whole bag of carrots!

She laughed as she petted him. He looked at her. His eyes were so big they seemed to take up his entire face.

She said, "OK. Mr. Donkey. I'll see you later."

What she didn't know is that he was going to become her good buddy – someone she quickly grew attached to.

Of all things.

She DID notice that she was noticing everything these days. The blue sky. The warm sun. The Donkey. The guitar player named Tony.

If she were dead she never would have seen any of it. She would have been in another world.

She headed back to the retreat center so she wouldn't be late.

Chapter 9 ~ The Blessing

Cheryl arrived back at the Edwene Gaines' retreat center Saturday afternoon with only a minute to spare before she would have been considered late. Edwene watched everybody as they arrived from their long afternoon break. Edwene was a beautiful woman who carried herself well. Her clothes reflected that, too.

"If I'm considered late, I'm blaming it on the Donkey. It's his fault," Cheryl said to herself.

But there was no need to blame anyone. Edwene welcomed everybody back and hoped they had a nice break.

The evening part was similar to the morning with people sharing more progress on identifying goals. Edwene reminded everyone that no matter what the goal was a *deadline* for completing it was critical. It didn't matter how far away the deadline was – weeks, months, or even a year.

What was important was that each person HAD a deadline. A specific date for completing their goal.

In Cheryl's case, it was to write a book in a month.

She was optimistic.

And probably unrealistic.

Edwene had a number of magazines, colored paper and markers to encourage people to be creative in making a vision poster. It was to be a visual representation of each person's goal. Whatever that was. She also gave out small token gifts to help with ideas for their posters. With each small gift she explained the meaning of each one.

At the end of a wonderful evening while others were cleaning up their areas, Cheryl noticed a piano against the wall. She asked Edwene if she could play it.

"Of course, Cher. Go ahead," said Edwene.

Cheryl played a song she learned when she was 12 years old. Her piano teacher, Miss Ethel Fennefos made her memorize it. Cheryl didn't think she could ever memorize it but Miss Fennefos kept insisting and believing in her.

Cheryl had memorized it and played the same arrangement of the song for over 40 years. She could play it in her sleep, totally exhausted. What changed over the years was how Cheryl put much more feeling into the exact same arrangement she learned as a 12 year old.

The song was, 'Somewhere Over the Rainbow' sung by Judy Garland in *'The Wizard of Oz'*. Judy was another Minnesotan. She had become quite famous for singing that song.

After playing the song, Cheryl looked over at Edwene, who was smiling.

Cheryl next played her version of Led Zeppelin's 'Stairway to Heaven' which her brother Jerry made her figure out on the piano at age 17. Jerry learned the guitar version of the song when he was 15 and in a rock band. As brother and sister they were only 2 years apart and very close friends.

He said to her back then, "Hey Cher. Figure out that Led Zeppelin song Stairway to Heaven so that we can play it together. You can do it."

Cheryl protested and said, "Jer, you've got to be kidding! I'll never figure that out. There are too many notes in it. It's too hard."

He had insisted just like Miss Ethel Fennefos had insisted – and Jer believed she could do it.

So she did. Because her brother believed she could do it.

Note by note she played the record over and over again on the turntable lifting the record needle to different parts of the song until she memorized it. There was never any published music for that song from Led Zeppelin so whenever she played it on the piano people seemed to be amazed. She even played Stairway to Heaven at the Woman's Club of Minneapolis during Sunday brunches.

The Baby Boomers loved it. She would play it between Beethoven and Chopin numbers. In an elegant setting like the Woman's Club of Minneapolis it worked.

The only other person she had ever heard play that song on the *piano* was Lorie Line -- another well known piano player who had gotten her start in the Twin Cities.

It was Lorie Line who suggested she get a piano again while married to Michael.

Cheryl lived without a piano for 20 years after she graduated from Irondale High School in New Brighton, got married and moved away with her first husband. There was no room for a piano at their cozy new trailer home in the Upper Peninsula of Michigan while he was in the Air Force. He was stationed at K.I. Sawyer Air Force Base on the peninsula.

It was after Cheryl got married a 2nd time to Michael that she met Lorie Line. She really missed the piano she grew up with.

Cheryl bought a piano because Lorie Line suggested she should. Just like that.

At a book signing in the Mall of America where Lorie was playing and marketing her song arrangements, Lorie told her, "Cheryl, I think you should get a piano again. You obviously love it."

Cheryl was buying Lorie's piano books without even owning a piano. She had explained it all to Lorie. Cheryl bought a brand new Yamaha piano the next week. She'd been playing ever since.

Cheryl's love of piano playing is what Edwene Gaines heard that Saturday night as people were cleaning up. Cheryl was lost in her own world. She had some of Lorie Line's arrangements with her that she played, too.

Everyone gradually drifted back to their hotels or homes or bed and breakfasts. Cheryl was one of the last to leave. She said goodbye to Edwene. As Edwene walked away into the night it suddenly struck her how much Edwene reminded her of Miss Ethel Fennefos.

Her childhood piano teacher Miss Fennefos and Edwene were the same!

Edwene was approximately the same size as what Cheryl remembered her piano teacher was and had the same bubbly personality. They both encouraged her. They both laughed a lot. They were both Funny.

Cheryl wondered if Miss Ethel Fennefos had come back somehow within Edwene.

Cheryl only took piano lessons through the 6th grade before Miss Fennefos retired. Miss Ethel Fennefos was old when Cheryl started taking lessons in 2nd grade. She was almost near retirement as Cheryl started.

Cheryl found out later that Miss Fennefos worked an extra year as a piano teacher in order to teach Cheryl. She told Cheryl's parents that Cheryl had a gift for playing that she had never seen in any of her students.

Miss Fennefos died a few years after that. She never married and seemed to love teaching piano.

Cheryl learned years later that Miss Fennefos was recommended by Cheryl's real-life Godmother, her Aunt LaVonne. Her aunt was married to Cheryl's mom's brother Alverne. It seemed appropriate that her real Godmother led a piano teacher to her that looked just like a Fairy Godmother.

In fact, her real Godmother Aunt LaVonne also looked like a Fairy Godmother from Cinderella.

Cheryl made a note to tell Edwene that story about Miss Fennefos the next day if she got a chance.

She found her way back to the Inn in the Woods. She was exhausted for the 3rd day in a row. It had been a long trip from Minneapolis to Chicago to Mentone. She was glad that she didn't have to be back until 9:30 am the next morning.

She remembered hearing the Tree Frogs as she went to sleep that night. At least she knew what they were. Rebecca even confirmed that it was what was making all the noise in the trees. The guy she met at the DeSoto rest stop was not on drugs after all.

On Sunday, Cheryl woke up around 6 am. No deer were outside her window that morning. She waited but none came.

It made the previous morning seem even more special.

She smelled fresh coffee. Her next door neighbor at the Inn was drinking it on the front porch. Cheryl got dressed to go outside. She met a woman named Nancy who was vacationing with her two young daughters. They struck up a conversation. Cheryl found out Nancy was recently divorced.

Cheryl was reminded what it was like to be divorced with young children. It was how her daughter Sarah was raised. Without a father living in the house. Cheryl divorced her first husband when Sarah was only 2 years old. She married her high school sweetheart, John, because she was in love with him.

She divorced him because their marriage was like the movie *'Grease'* starring Olivia Newton-John and John Travolta. Two people wildly attracted to each other but vastly different. It doesn't work in the long run.

In the movie *'Grease'* both characters try to change each other. Neither one wins.

Years later Cheryl found out that John Travolta ~ the actor in *'Grease'* ~ was only 2 weeks older than she was. She saw him on the cover of People magazine right before he turned 50. It's also how she found out Oprah was close to the same age as her. When famous people are on the cover of People magazine turning 50 you notice things like that.

At this stage in her life Cheryl did not regret marrying her husband, John. She got a daughter out of the deal who she loved very much. She wouldn't have traded that for anything. Thanks to Sally and Greg's wedding, she now had a daughter who was in her thirties and doing very well as an e-Learning software trainer. Sarah soaked up new software like a sponge.

Cheryl explained all of this to Nancy while they shared coffee together. Both women walked to breakfast together with the young girls.

As Cheryl sat down to the table, she noticed her napkin holder was a Dragonfly. She gasped.

"What the ---?!!'"

She looked around at the other napkin holders. All of them were different. Hers was the only one that was a Dragonfly. She smiled. She was turning into a Dragonfly herself by stopping to notice things. Without moving.

After another spirited conversation with the guests that morning, Cheryl stayed a bit longer to talk to Rebecca. She thanked her again for another gluten-free exquisite breakfast. Rebecca was really trying to be accommodating.

As she helped Rebecca clean up Cheryl was focused on the time. She knew that she couldn't be late. Edwene wanted people to be there by 9:30. Sharp. No excuses.

Cheryl found herself telling Rebecca about her current situation. What had happened on July 15. How she had found herself in a screaming match with her husband just a few days before which prompted her to suddenly take off for Alabama.

Cheryl told Rebecca in confidence some of the other things about her marriage to Michael, which she probably shouldn't have. She admitted to dealing with many Rage issues from Michael over the previous 20 years.

It was a conversation that was going to come back to haunt her. Something she had to learn the hard way.

Don't tell strangers things about your life that might scare them.

Cheryl left in what she thought was plenty of time to get to Edwene's Valley Head retreat center. This time she was driving by herself because the other two women had taken off. She went down one dirt road to another.

Before she realized it she was totally lost.

"Oh no!!! I'll be late!! Edwene will be upset!!"

She backtracked along the dirt roads and tried frantically to figure out where she was. There were no street signs. All of the beautiful pasture fields looked alike to her. Especially when lost. It was all a bunch of fields with white fences. Beautiful fields with white fences but scary when you're lost.

And Late.

She turned around again and started back. Finally she came to a point where she noticed familiar wooden signs. She had not taken a left down a dirt road where she should have. So she quickly turned right down that road and sailed along. She came into Mentone and then knew how to get to the retreat from there.

Her heart was racing as she tried to make up for lost time. She was driving like Mario Andretti again down the mountain from Mentone. This time by herself.

She saw the donkey to her right as she flew down the last dirt road. She heard the Donkey call out when he saw her car, 'BRAHH UHH! BRAHHHHHHH UHH!'

She slammed to a stop. He looked lonely. She patted his head and gave him some more carrots. Then she apologized for having to leave again but told him she'd be back.

She was getting attached to a donkey. Even talking to him. In northern Alabama. How crazy was that? If he wasn't so darn cute.

As she arrived at the center she ran as fast as she could to the main building but found nobody there. She ran to the meditation room. It was already in progress. The time was a few minutes past 9:30 am. She was out of breath.

Maybe others will come after me. Like yesterday. She hoped. But nobody did. She was the last one in the room.

By her calculations, she figured she was about 5 minutes late. She really WAS late, though. No doubt about it. She saw Edwene look at her as she tried to slip unobtrusively into the meditation room. She tried to melt against the side wall so Edwene wouldn't see her.

"I hate being late." She said to herself. "It seems I'm always trying to do one more thing and one more thing. One of these days I'll get a handle on Time."

After another wonderful meditation session Cheryl saw Edwene look directly at her.

Cheryl avoided Edwene's gaze and started a conversation with two other women on the way back to the main building. Cheryl was in the middle of a conversation with them when Edwene came up to her and hooked Cheryl's little finger on her left hand.

Edwene said to her sweetly, "Cher will you come with me outside for a moment?"

"Sure." She replied in a low voice, not a happy one.

Oh no! Thought Cheryl. I knew it. I'm going to get yelled at for being late. If it *wasn't* for that d---n donkey I would have been on time. I *never* should have talked to Rebecca from the Inn in the Woods that long. If *only* I hadn't gotten lost!!

Cheryl was beating herself up internally and her heart sank as Edwene took her outside the large glass doors of the retreat center to the patio. She could tell everybody in the center could see that she was with Edwene. The sliding glass doors and windows were huge. She hated getting chastised for being late. It happened to her often.

As Edwene turned towards Cheryl, she unhooked her little finger and smiled. Cheryl braced herself.

What Edwene said to her was something Cheryl never expected.

Edwene said, "Cher, I had a dream about you last night."

Cheryl thought to herself, "Oh no. She dreamt I was going to be late. And I was. Of course. She must be psychic. She must have known I have a hard time being on Time. I hate it when I'm late."

Her heart sank further. She did not want to let Edwene down by being inconsiderate. And Late.

But that's not what Edwene said.

Edwene continued with, "I have to tell you that in all the hundreds of seminars I've done over the last 20 years and the thousands of people I've met, I've never dreamt about *any* of my participants before. But I had a dream last night that I was supposed to bless you today. Do I have your permission to bless you this morning?"

Cheryl was having a tough time comprehending what Edwene was saying because it was so far from what she was expecting.

Her mind was racing. She heard numbers. Hundreds and thousands???? Over 20 years? That sounded like a *lot*.

Her mind was temporarily distracted by calculations. Followed by the echo of Edwene's words, "permission to bless you …"

What the ----?!

Cheryl found herself saying, "Huh? Uh sure. Of course. You have my permission."

How could this be? Even after she was LATE! But only by a couple of minutes. This was not happening. This couldn't possibly be happening.

What in the world was going on? Was she imagining it? How was that possible? She was *not* going to get chastised! Was she losing her mind? Did she hear that right?

Cheryl was barely comprehending what she was hearing as Edwene continued with, "So when we go back into this room I will announce to everybody that I am going to bless you outside in a special circle. Are you OK with that?"

"Sure. No problem," said Cheryl numbly and slowly as if she was frozen. She was completely in shock.

Huh??

Cheryl was still feeling frozen when Edwene led her back into the room. Her mind was racing. How come she didn't get punished for being late? Who was this woman? Why did she remind Cheryl so much of Miss Ethel Fennefos, the piano teacher she loved so much?

Her piano teacher looked like the Fairy Godmother in Walt Disney's Cinderella movie. Miss Fennefos was always giggling, it seemed. So was Edwene. They both had a sense of Humor. They both must be Smart.

They both had that Fairy Godmother look about them.

Edwene announced to the group that she was going to take everybody outside and offer a blessing to 'Cher'. Cheryl felt embarrassed. She didn't know what to expect. She was not only *very* late the first night (Friday) by not showing up at all, she was late to the previous two morning meditation sessions. By a few minutes.

It didn't make sense to her. Nothing made sense anymore. Why didn't she get punished?

She didn't deserve to be treated this well.

But Cheryl was not in charge. Edwene was.

Edwene took all the participants outside to the patio overlooking the beautiful Alabama valley. They didn't call it Valley Head for nothing. The area was truly breath-takingly beautiful. It was the

Head of a Valley. Or something like that. That's what was going through Cheryl's mind as they were ushered outside. It was the only way she could remember the name of the place she was at.

As the group formed a circle on the patio in the sunshine, Edwene told Cher to get into the middle of the circle.

Then she said to the group, "I know many of you are going through difficult times, so I'd like 3 of you to join Cher in the circle."

"Thank God. I'm not the only one," Cheryl thought. "That makes it easier. I still don't deserve to be blessed. This can't be happening."

Immediately 3 other people stepped into the circle. Edwene stood behind Cheryl and put her hands on her shoulders. She offered a blessing for Cheryl. Then Edwene blessed each of the other 3 in the circle by placing her hands on *their* shoulders.

The experience was so powerful for Cheryl who was expecting to get chastised for being late, that she started crying.

She had tears streaming down her face as she looked out over the beautiful valley thinking, "If I were dead I'd never be experiencing this. This is unbelievable. I can't handle this. It's so far from where I was a month ago. I felt utterly worthless then and now I'm being honored."

Again, she realized the retreat would still be happening if she were dead, but she wouldn't have been there to experience it.

After all 4 people were blessed, Edwene told them to rejoin the circle and have 4 others come into the middle of the circle. So they did. And then 4 more were blessed. And so on until the entire circle of 20 people were blessed.

At the end of the blessing, Edwene told them all to make a large circle again. As they did, Cheryl noticed that her name tag had come off and was in the middle of the circle on the patio. Cheryl cried out, "Oh No! Let me get that!"

To which Edwene replied, "No, Cher, leave it there. It's appropriate that your name be in the center of the circle."

Cheryl thought, "I'm overwhelmed. I don't deserve this. This is just too much. It's too far from where I was a month ago for me to handle this. I was worthless a month ago. What happened?"

Finally, the blessing was over. Everyone went inside.

Cheryl picked up her name tag from the wooden patio and realized she couldn't relate to her married name anymore. She was no longer that person. She wanted to go back to her maiden name of Lindberg. And change her first name legally to Cher.

She wanted to leave the old Cheryl behind. Completely.

And so she did.

From then on she *really* became Cher. The same name her family had called her since she was a teenager.

Just like her younger brother Ter and other brother Jer. Before there was another Cher.

Chapter 10 ~ Playing with Fire

It took Cher quite a while to get back into the Moment after Edwene's blessing. Her mind was racing. She had been caught off guard so much that it was hard for her to process anything.

How could she have gone from feeling totally worthless a month ago to being highly regarded and blessed? By a strange woman she didn't know in the middle of Nowhere?

The Northeastern corner of Alabama to be exact but it felt like a different planet to her.

It could have just as well been Mars or the Moon. Nothing was making any sense to her.

After a while she calmed down and started focusing again on clarifying her goal. There were more exercises to do and more writing. She had gotten to know some of the other people attending the seminar and could relate to some of their goals.

Cher came back to the Present Moment as Edwene was talking about that evening's activity.

She couldn't believe what she was hearing. Edwene was describing walking on red-hot coals as an *optional* activity for each person to do. Only if they were ready. Nobody had to do it.

What??!!! I never signed up for this. Where did it say that?? I'm NOT going to do that! I don't care that I've been blessed. Somebody in this group has to have some sense.

It's going to have to be me.

Edwene asked for a show of hands on how many had walked on coals with her before. A total of 14 hands went up.

All these people have walked on coals??!!! Only 6 out of 20 in the group had *never* walked on coals before with this woman? How could this be?!!

The others who had done this before smiled knowingly at those who had not.

Cher was mystified at the Inner Look that the group who had done this coal-walk thing gave to the group who had not.

What was up with that???!! Who were these crazy people?

But Edwene made it clear that nobody was expected to do the fire walk on coals that Sunday night. They had to be ready to do it.

Ready to do what!!??

And then she saw them.

The t-shirts hanging up on the wall of the retreat center that were labeled 'Firewalker'. One was an awesome combination of red, orange and yellow colors. It caught her eye.

If I do this crazy fire-walking thing, then I can buy the t-shirt.

It's awesome!

However, the words of her father came to her immediately after she realized that she wanted the t-shirt. His words that she grew up with were: "Don't do something just because everybody around you is doing it. If they were all jumping off a cliff, would you?"

Her dad said this often. It prevented her from doing lots of things her friends were doing. She was an independent thinker. She did not get caught up in doing drugs or skipping out of school or anything else that her friends thought was 'cool'.

Her dad believed in her.

He believed and encouraged her to play the piano. He gave her credit for getting straight 'A's in school. He *really* wanted her to go to college – especially since *he* had not. One thing that was ingrained in her growing up was that continuous learning was a valuable thing.

Her dad was always reading books and volunteering for President of something. Like President of the PTA (Parent Teachers Association) while she was in grade school at Sunnyside or President of Toastmasters or the President of the Marco Island Historical Society.

What was unusual about him being in leadership roles was that he started out as a truck driver for Land O' Lakes. A cross-eyed truck driver, no less. He was born with crossed-eyes, so as a young child one eye took over the other and he became blind in one eye. He grew up with this stigma.

The pictures of him at close range indicated this disability. His high school picture had one eye roaming at an angle, making him look a bit odd.

He told her that sometimes people looked down on him as he was growing up because they considered him Stupid. But he was not. It was only his appearance that made him look like that. He was completely normal. He couldn't help it that he was born with crossed-eyes.

While she was listening to Edwene and trying to decide what to do about walking on fire, Cher flashed on the memory of when she was 3 years old. Her dad had been reading about a new eye operation. It was from the Mayo Clinic or the University of Minnesota, she couldn't remember.

At any rate, her dad decided that he would have this new operation done. The operation to 'uncross' his eyes. The surgeon magically attached the muscles of his blind eye to track the muscles of his good eye.

The result was that his eyes moved around together. The blind eye no longer wandered as a crossed-eye.

He looked normal. He was still blind in one eye, but he looked normal.

His career at Land O'Lakes took off.

He was Funny and Smart. He often made everybody around him laugh with Scandinavian Ole and Lena jokes. He was someone Cher was truly proud of. Especially since he had come so far in his life – not only in his career from Truck Driver to Manager but also by marrying two women he loved and suffering through their deaths.

Then recovering from both deaths. Of women he had loved.

Cher remembered how as a little girl she saw him come home from the hospital with a black patch on his eye. She asked her dad what was wrong, and he said, "Don't worry Cheryl. I'll be fine. My eye has been fixed."

This is what Cher remembered as she was in Alabama contemplating whether or not to do the fire-walking exercise Edwene was describing to the 20 people at the seminar.

She admired her dad for all the ridicule and pain he must have suffered growing up. He didn't let other people's opinions influence him.

"I don't have to do this just because everybody else is doing it. I appreciate the fact I've been blessed, but so has everybody else. I'm not under any obligation to do anything. Edwene has made that very clear." Cher said to herself.

"Edwene didn't say one word about the t-shirts hanging on the wall in her retreat center. I happened to notice them on my own."

She came back to the present Moment after pondering all these things to hear Edwene talk about the last little gift she had for everyone in the group.

It was a small Dragonfly.

Cheryl gasped and said out loud, "Oh no!!"

Everyone looked at her. She felt embarrassed for the 2nd time that day and apologized to the group.

What is going on??!!! I've been fascinated by Dragonflies for the last several weeks. I am becoming one. And now Edwene has given these out with an explanation of why dragonflies are important.

It was too much for her to comprehend.

***

TREA$URE YOUR LIFE

Later that night the burning coals of a fire had been carefully prepared. The participants had been watching it burn on the back lawn most of the afternoon.

Edwene started it out by walking on the coals. She had to walk about 10 feet on the red-hot coals. One by one others followed. Cher watched nearly everyone in the group do it. Even Anna, the woman from New Jersey who was her fellow guest at the Inn in the Woods was brave enough to do it. Anna did it twice.

Twice!!! In the same night.

"Boy those people from New Jersey sure have guts," thought Cher. "Either that or they are totally crazy."

"That's it." She said to herself. "I'm going to try it. I really do want that t-shirt."

Cher went to the coals twice and chickened out both times.

She said to herself, "Don't do this just because everybody else is doing it. The t-shirt is not worth it. Remember what your father said to you. If everybody you knew were jumping off a cliff, would you do it?"

"Besides, you don't have health insurance anymore. You don't have a job. If you burn your feet this could be disaster for you."

She stood outside the crowd.

But then she heard the train whistle in the distance. It was the same train she heard as she was going into Mentone just a few days before.

It was saying to her, "It's OK. Don't worry. You'll be alright."

So as one of the last participants to walk on coals that night she stepped up to the coals, looked Edwene in the eye and went for it.

She walked the 10 feet on hot coals. It was painless. Except for the last step. She remembered feeling that her left foot was a bit hot but then a bucket of cold water was the relief.

What Edwene told the group ahead of time was that if they had the Spiritual guidance to know they could do this, their lives would never be the same. How scary could anything be if they knew they had walked on coals?

Edwene made it clear that *nobody* was expected to do it, and if people weren't ready, they should not. Nobody was going to be chastised for not going along with it. Sometimes even *Edwene* did not do it with her group. One had to be in the right frame of mind.

Cher was exhilarated beyond belief! She walked on red hot coals and survived! Without any burns at all!

What was up with that?!!

Now I can get that Firewalker t-shirt!

Chapter 11 ~ Staying in Mentone?

After walking on coals and purchasing the Firewalker t-shirt she earned, Cher felt stronger. She was more confident, exhilarated and grateful to be alive. Especially without any burns on her feet. No trip to the emergency room for her!

She was again astonished when Edwene said to the entire group afterwards, "This was the *hottest* fire I've ever walked on. I almost told you after I walked it, DO NOT do this. But then I figured I'd made it clear that everybody had their own choice. Nobody was going to be chastised for *not* doing it. It was up to you."

The *hottest* fire Edwene had ever done? How can a fire be *more* than *hot*?? Isn't hot the most hottest thing?

Cher wondered.

The retreat ended Sunday night. Cher had gotten to know some of the people quite well over the previous few days. She exchanged phone numbers and promised to stay in touch.

She said goodbye to Edwene. It was hard to leave such a beautiful lady but Cher knew she had to go back home and face her Husband.

Cher did not see Mr. Donkey on her way back to the Inn in the Woods. It was dark. She wondered where he went at night. She remembered asking some of the other participants that night if they had seen the donkey.

"Donkey – what donkey?" They all asked her. Everyone she mentioned it to said the same thing.

There is a donkey around here?

"Yes, I'm sure of it. I even have pictures. Didn't anybody see it?"

Nobody had.

In order to see the Donkey one had to become a Dragonfly and actually stop moving.

For the 4th day in a row she fell into bed totally exhausted. This time she was also exhilarated. And calm. She didn't know exactly what she was going to do next. She knew that checkout from the Inn was scheduled for Monday morning at 11 am. It was clearly marked on the door.

She fell asleep wondering if she could stay just a few more days…

* * *

The next morning she woke up early – her usual 5 am time. She didn't see any deer and didn't hear anybody else walking around.

She got up and thought, "I wonder if Rebecca has this room rented for the rest of the week. If not, I'd love to stay longer. I'll just sell some more of my Scottrade IRA stock. I'm almost out of money in my checking account. I only have enough gas money to get back to Minnesota."

"But I'm not ready to go back yet and face Michael. I need more time."

So, Cher came up with a Plan. After all, her dad was a Planner and he did not do anything without a Plan.

Her Plan was to ask Rebecca if she could stay a few more days. That was the next Plan. At least until the end of the week.

First she went on an exploratory walk. The morning light was barely up. It was 6 am. She started off in a different direction than she had from the previous morning and was surprised to find more enchanting buildings.

One was a small church. Actually a really *tiny* church. It was beautiful to see this nestled in the woods.

As Cher was walking around the church she decided to check her emails from her Blackberry phone. She was surprised to find an email from her E-circle. This was the same group of women who had rejected her so many months before. Her E-circle from the Woman Within organization. Why were they sending *her* an email?

She realized after she read it that one of the women must have picked up an old email that still had Cher's email address on it. And inadvertently replied to everyone.

It was a fairly normal email, talking about how the particular woman couldn't be at the E-circle meeting that week. At first, Cher felt a pang in her heart at not being included in the Woman Within circle anymore. This was followed by a feeling of strength, confidence and exhilaration at walking on coals the night before.

Like Edwene said, "Once you do this you will never feel the same again."

After giving it a couple of minutes thought, she decided to respond to everyone on the list. The entire Woman Within E-circle. She copied them all within the same email so they knew she was simply replying to the message sent to her by mistake.

She typed in her email note:

> "Thank you all for being there for so many years while I was in your E-circle. I have valued your friendship. I've decided that I do NOT need to return to this group. I do NOT need a year of professional therapy as you all insisted on. I'm doing just fine.
>
> I am living my life joyously and intend to keep doing that in the future. Good luck to all of you."

She felt *great* after sending this message!! It took a load off her mind. One less thing left hanging in her life. She really did *not* need a year of therapy to return to their group. Who were they to dictate those kinds of conditions on her anyway??! They weren't psychiatrists! Who was behind it all??

She figured she knew who it was.

What was up with that?!!

She found out many months later that shortly after she sent the email, her E-circle group stopped meeting. It completely disbanded.

If she had spent the money on therapy for a year in order to get back into the E-circle, it would have been for nothing.

She checked another email message on her phone. It was from the captain of her bowling team at the U of MN. This was a team she took over as captain 15 years before while working at the University Computer Center – known as UCC.

TREA$URE YOUR LIFE | 177

UCC (University Computer Center) were the same initials as her Unity Christ Church in Golden Valley – also known as UCC.

She and Michael often joked about that because they met while working at UCC - the University Computer Center. Michael did not go to her UCC church at all, except when Cher absolutely insisted.

Like special holidays or when she was playing the piano in front of the congregation.

At any rate, she saw the note from James, the captain of her bowling team, asking who would be back again this year to bowl. Even though she was no longer employed by the University, she could still bowl in the league if she bowled continuously without any 6 month lapses. Those were the league bylaws.

She bowled once a month to stay in touch with her old colleagues.

She saw the note from James on her Blackberry and thought about it. It was August. This was typical of James or any captain to send out a message. Cher remembered she had given up being Captain to James when she was severely depressed over being laid off from the University.

James took control as Captain of her team called 'More Than Enough' and kept the team going. The only problem Cher had with James was that he exhibited inappropriate anger while bowling. He would throw his towel against the floor or swear at himself for getting a split. He'd work himself into a Rage for not bowling as well as he could have.

James did not take his anger out on the rest of the team, but it was annoying that he worked himself into such a Rage. Over bowling?

It was supposed to be a fun league.

It occurred to her at that moment that James was *just like her Husband, Michael,* and his inappropriate Rage!! It was nerve-racking.

As she sat beside the wonderful little church in Alabama, she decided to respond to James with the following message from her phone:

> "James, thank you so much for taking over as Captain of our team during a time when I was struggling. You have kept the team going. Unfortunately, I won't be coming back to bowl with your team. I'm going to become a Free Agent.
>
> I will be looking for another team to bowl on. The best of luck to you. See you at bowling!"

Again, she felt great! It was exhilarating to move on! She figured she'd have no problem getting on another bowling team. She knew practically everybody who bowled at the U and had been bowling for the last 20 years. People were always looking for more players.

She wound up joining a really fun team later ~ The Jacks and Queens.

She was free to live her life again! As God wanted her to.

She was making choices to get out of difficult situations. She had her confidence back that had gotten buried over the years.

She walked back to the Inn in the Woods with new awareness.

After another wonderful homemade breakfast from Rebecca, Cher cautiously approached Rebecca after the other guests left. All the guests were leaving Monday morning.

Cher asked Rebecca, "Would it be possible for me to stay a few more days?"

To which Rebecca immediately and curtly replied, "No, it is not. I'm leaving for Atlanta today to visit my dad who is not doing well."

Cher restated her desire to stay a few more days. She told Rebecca that she would go somewhere else for breakfast every morning. She needed a place to stay and was not ready to go back to Minnesota. Cher even offered to watch the place while Rebecca was away.

"No, that is not possible. Due to liability issues I cannot have you here while I'm gone."

That made some sense to Cher.

But then Rebecca went on to explain in a really curt tone that she was really worried about Cher's husband, Michael. She was concerned that he might try to come down to Alabama and physically hurt Cher and possibly Rebecca.

Cher was shocked. "What?!!! Michael would never do that!!"

Her conversation from the day before flashed in her mind. She never should have told Rebecca the things she said about what Michael had done to her. Physically. In his Rage.

Cher went on to explain to Rebecca: "He gets angry and upset and Rageful but his anger is like striking a match. He feels bad about it immediately afterwards. He's not the type who would plan such a thing. He has no time for me. He's too busy with his work. He's the only one bringing in any money. I've been an Information

Technology Consultant but right now I'm out of work. So he's paying the bills and the mortgage. I'm bringing in nothing."

Cher tried desperately to explain all this to Rebecca but it fell on deaf ears. Cher noticed a police car outside the window.

"What's that for?" Cher asked.

Rebecca said it was a precaution. She had called him to make sure Cher checked out of the Inn in the Woods.

What the ----??!!!

Cher hadn't seen a police car the entire time she had been in Mentone. She didn't even know they had one.

Cher gave up and resigned herself to leave the Inn in the Woods. She remembered what she told Rebecca the day before.

She never should have confided these things to a complete stranger, no matter how nice the stranger appeared.

Their conversation came back to haunt her.

As she packed up and left the Inn she thought, "Now what am I going to do? This town is only two blocks long and it's not like I can just go to a hotel."

Or can I?

She remembered the 4-way stop sign at the top of the mountain in Mentone. On one side was The Mentone Inn and the other side was The Mentone Springs Hotel. She figured one of those places had to have a room available for the rest of the week.

So she headed out from the Inn in the Woods under estranged circumstances. She wanted to remember the place as a wonderful magical place. She had learned a lot.

Both Rebecca and the police car were watching her as she left.

She drove back to Mentone and parked at The Mentone Inn. There was plenty of parking available. Nobody's car was in the lot.

That's strange, she thought. Nobody's here? There were lots of cars in the parking lot on Friday night when I got here and thought it was the right place.

She went up to the door of The Mentone Inn and found a note that said: 'CLOSED. ON VACATION THIS WEEK.'

Drat.

She walked across the street to The Mentone Springs Hotel and found the same type of note. It was also CLOSED FOR THE WEEK.

What the ----??!!!

The only two hotels in town were closed for the week!? What was up with that???!!

It felt like a Ghost Town.

The town was only two blocks long. Both hotels were closed. During the same week.

Cher sat on the steps of The Mentone Springs Hotel feeling totally dejected. She didn't want to go back to Minnesota yet. She had no job to go back to. She had been talking to her Dad who knew she'd be driving back to Chicago and spending that night with him. He was expecting her to leave Mentone that morning. Monday morning.

So was Michael. Her Husband.

When she arrived in Mentone a few days before on Friday night, this place was magical. It was filled with wonderful music of a family getting ready for a wedding. In what was like a surreal movie setting of a timeless and elegant hotel.

Now the sun was shining and everybody was gone. Had she imagined the people??

Sitting on the steps of The Mentone Springs Hotel, she looked across the street at The Mentone Inn. And the St. Joseph's on the Mountain Episcopal Church next to it.

It was Noon. Nobody was around. No sign of life in the entire town.

Has everybody died? She felt totally alone.

And then she heard them. The bells from the church across the street.

The church bells were striking Noon. Twelve of them. As each bell struck in the deserted town it echoed magnificently off the buildings. She remembered the words of Edwene from the night before: "Your life will never be the same after you have walked on coals. Don't do it if you're not ready. You are dealing with Fire. Believe in Yourself. Trust in God."

The church bells were saying to her: *"Look across the street. You'll find the answer."*

If she had gone right past the 4-way stop at the top of the mountain on her way to the Inn in the Woods Friday night, she would not have had the experience of the musical family practicing for the wedding rehearsal at The Mentone Springs Hotel. She wouldn't have noticed there were two hotels in town. She would have driven right past them.

Was that a dream?

She would *not* be sitting on the steps of The Mentone Springs Hotel wondering what to do next.

She needed more Time.

She turned into a Dragonfly. She looked across the street while sitting on the steps of The Mentone Springs Hotel listening to the noon bells. After a few moments she noticed a guy working in the St. Joseph's church yard off in the distance.

A Human!! What are the odds?!! There is Life around here!

She walked across the street and met a wonderful man named Harry. He looked like a Harry. Tall and lanky and older.

She explained her situation being very careful not to mention anything about Michael's rage that might intimidate him. She only said she had a wonderful time attending Edwene Gaines' seminar.

He knew who Edwene was.

She told him she didn't want to go back to Minnesota yet because she was falling in love with the area and wanted to experience it more. But she needed a place to stay. She explained that both hotels were closed for the week.

Harry said, "You know, there's a place close by. Can't remember the name of it but it has great gardens. Lots of flowers. You might like it. The lady in the church office knows where it is."

A place close by with flowers?!!! There's a church lady in the office? Another Human? Cher was a gardener and loved flowers. She spent many years organizing the annual Prospect Park Garden Walk.

Cher would explain to people, "It's not that the Gardens walk in Prospect Park, it's that people walk to the gardens."

Some thought that was Funny.

So she went into the church office and found a nice lady working there. It was a relief to find Human Beings in this ghost town. Thank God for the church bells!

She never would have heard them if she hadn't turned into a Dragonfly for those few moments.

She explained her situation to Alice who was quick to recognize the place Harry referred to. It was called the Raven Haven. About 15 minutes away. Alice looked up the phone number.

Cher called the number and a gentleman answered. His name was Tony, the proprietor. He said, "Yes, we do have 1 room available. But only for 3 days. Then we're booked solid for 2 weeks. We also only take *cash* or credit cards, *no checks*."

"I'll take it!" she replied.

Whoa!@!@! At this point in her life, 3 days were better than nothing!

She left the church feeling exhilarated!

Chapter 12 ~ Learning to Live

After talking to Tony the Raven Haven proprietor, Cher walked back to her car from the St. Joseph's Episcopal Church with excitement in every part of her body. She was going to *get* to stay a few more days in Mentone!!

The sun was shining and it was a beautiful warm summer day. She didn't have to go back to Minnesota and face Michael yet! She could stay in this part of Alabama and enjoy the scenery.

All of a sudden she realized she was out of money to pay for a bed and breakfast she had just booked for 3 days!! At a place that only accepted cash or credit cards. She had no credit cards anymore because they were all maxed out due to her layoff from the U.

How had she managed to do that?? This was *not* part of the original Plan.

She felt like an Idiot. What the ---??!

She had barely enough gas money in her checking account to drive back to Minneapolis. It was her only cash. She did not have the credit line backup on her checking account anymore either. It was maxed out.

Hmmmm…

She didn't want to call her Dad and ask him for money. He'd probably say No because it wasn't part of the Plan. She was supposed to leave Monday for Chicago. That Moment. Around Noon.

She also didn't want to ask Michael for it. He would also probably say No because he never wanted her to go to Alabama in the first place.

Who in the world could she call?

She sat back on the steps of The Mentone Springs Hotel. To think.

As a Dragonfly...

The same hotel steps she was sitting on opened a door for her Friday night. It was where the musical family had been singing for the wedding rehearsal dinner. Because of their rehearsal dinner she was able to find the directions to her Inn in the Woods. Was that a dream?

She didn't think so. Even though The Mentone Springs Hotel was closed on a Monday morning with nobody around, she was sure it was full of people Friday night at Midnight. It was magical.

After thinking about all her possibilities to ask someone for money she decided to take a chance.

A really *scary* chance for her. But somewhat creative of an idea. She was afraid of rejection.

She picked up her Blackberry and located the number for Mike Paxton, one of her piano students. He was the former CEO of some companies in the Minneapolis area. He had been taking piano lessons from her for a few years. She figured he might have some money.

Cher called Mike on his cell phone and explained the situation. She asked if he could advance her $250 for future piano lessons and wire it to her checking account immediately so she could stay in

Alabama longer. She promised to teach him the lessons in the future.

He agreed to do it saying he didn't often loan people money. Even to *his own daughters*. He told her he would make an exception in her case under the circumstances. His wife, Sue would take care of the details.

"Whoo-Hoo!! Thanks! That's all I need for now!" She told him. He laughed.

She figured it would take care of the bed and breakfast plus food she would need over the next few days. She called Sue and gave her the checking account information.

It would also give her some time to sell some Scottrade IRA stock as a safety net.

From the steps of The Mentone Springs Hotel she first called her Dad. He was the one expecting her to leave that day from Alabama and drive straight through to Chicago. She told him she'd be in Alabama for at least 3 more days. He wondered why? How could she do that without any money or a job? That wasn't part of the Plan.

She assured him it was OK. She would sell some more of her IRA stock. She didn't tell him about the money Mike was going to wire to her checking account. Her dad knew Mike personally and would *not* be pleased. She explained that she was not ready to go back to Michael. She needed more time to think about stuff.

He sounded reluctant. He didn't really know what was going on with her marriage. She was not following the Plan for coming back to his house as scheduled, but he finally agreed to her decision.

After all, he could no longer control his Daughter. She was 57 years old.

The next person she called was her husband, Michael.

She explained to him that she was not ready to come back to Minnesota. She needed more time to experience Alabama. Michael was not very open to the idea either – but he also realized Cheryl was out of *his* control. Even as his Wife, he could no longer tell her what to do. He wondered how she'd pay for another few days in Alabama.

"Don't worry, Michael. I'm cashing in some IRA stock. I'll be fine."

He grumbled about it but let her make the decision. He still didn't know about her near suicide. He only recognized that she had been acting very differently ever since he came back from his Guys Weekend. She had her old confidence back. He appreciated that. No more depression. That was progress.

Next she called her workout partner, Sheridan. "Sher, I'm still in Alabama and think I'll be staying for a few more days. You'll just have to continue working out by yourself until I get back."

Sheridan was the *only* one who supported her decision. "OK, Cher. Although I'll miss working out with you, I do understand. Stay as long as you have to. I'll see you when you get back."

She found out later that he did not work out at Bally's the whole time she was in Alabama. He didn't go to the club at all without her.

Cher drove back through the countryside around Mentone on her way to the Raven Haven Bed and Breakfast. She was once again exhilarated!! She thanked God for Mike Paxton being in her life. And she thanked God for Anastasia who introduced her to Mike. This wasn't the first time Mike had come through for her.

She remembered another time 2 years before when she was very depressed and thinking about jumping off the Franklin Ave Bridge in Minneapolis while the Mississippi River was partially frozen and covered in snow. It was one of those days that she felt particularly worthless. She figured after she hit the River she would be instantly frozen and it would be painless.

Mike had no idea what she was going through.

While thinking about jumping off the Franklin Ave Bridge, Mike Paxton interrupted her thoughts with a phone call that said, "So are we *on* for tonight?"

Meaning: Are we *on* for a piano lesson at his house in Minnetrista? A beautiful suburb located west of Minneapolis.

Cher answered automatically without even thinking about it – "Oh yeah, Mike. Of course. I'll be there."

It saved her life that day. It gave her a Purpose. She committed to giving him a piano lesson instead of taking her own Life. She didn't tell him about it until many months later.

Cher absolutely loved giving piano lessons to people. Including Mike.

The next week things had improved for her. When she called Mike the following Monday to confirm a piano lesson, he told her, "Oh Cheryl, I'm so sorry. I forgot to call you today and let you know I'm flying off to London tonight. I won't be there."

No problem.

If Mike Paxton had flown to London the week before and not called her, she could very possibly have followed through with her plan to jump off the Franklin Ave bridge. It was hard to say for sure. She felt as if she didn't matter to anyone.

Not even to her Husband, Michael.

At that time in her Life, she had no Job and no Purpose. She was in between contracting jobs and nothing mattered to her anymore. She was tired of having to prove herself all over again after having a successful career.

She was tired of dealing with Bullying and insecure Women in the workplace. She had no problems with men and with women who were confident and supportive. But the few women she ran into who were insecure and jealous types were trouble for her.

She thought about these things as she followed the directions exactly to the Raven Haven Bed and Breakfast. It seemed appropriate that Mike the CEO had come through for her again. Only this time she wasn't depressed.

It took her 15 minutes to get there. Just like the church lady said it would.

She rang the bell at a beautiful house. An older gentleman named Tony answered it. Cher explained that she was the one who had just called him.

Tony had one room available. It was called the Prairie Room.

"Prairie Room?" She asked.

"Yes, it is decorated with things from the prairie. Do you want do see it?"

"Of course," she answered.

She was led into what was formerly a garage on this fine house. It had been remodeled into a guest bedroom. Cher saw a wonderful bed, a cozy looking fireplace and a huge room. It had a Prairie Room look and feel to it. She felt right at home.

It even had an old fashioned train set in the window! A train set! What a coincidence.

She loved trains!

"I'll take it!" She said happily.

She was set for the next 3 days. She explained to Tony that she needed to get some cash from an ATM machine out of her checking account. He was fine with that. He told her where the only ATM machine was in town ~ at the Mentone Market down the road.

Cher got unpacked in her new Prairie Room and settled in for another 3 days in beautiful Mentone, Northeastern Alabama. The Middle of Nowhere.

She decided to explore the surrounding area. She took off in her silver Toyota Corolla. She headed to the place Tony told her about for the ATM machine ~ the Mentone Market. It was a charming, quaint store that reminded her of a 7/11 or PDQ market.

Except this place was different.

It had a small town feel. Everybody who stopped in seemed to know everybody else. The Mentone Market was where people got groceries and gas. And, as Tony said, it had the only ATM for miles around.

The red and gray tiles on the floor looked like a 50's style hamburger place. It had a long table and other chairs for people to sit at. In a grocery store?? How odd was that?

Cher called Fran from outside the market.

Cher explained that she was staying a few more days in Alabama because she just couldn't leave. And she was not ready to face Michael yet.

Fran said, "Where are you again in Alabama? What is the name of that town?"

Cheryl couldn't remember the name of the town so said, "I have no idea. It's something like Mentown."

Then she looked up at the name on the Mentone Market sign. Cher studied it for a moment. As a piano player she was used to taking apart chords and figuring out what the notes were. She took apart the name. Men ~ tone. She got it.

"Fran, the name of the town is Men ~ tone." She paused between each syllable.

On the spot she made up a phrase to her friend, "Men ~ Tone: Where the Men are Toned…. And the Women are Strong."

Fran laughed.

Cher had grown up in Minnesota, home of the mythical Lake Wobegon of Garrison Keillor. One of the more famous lines on his weekly radio show was, "That's the news from Lake Wobegon – Where the Women are Strong, the Men are Good-Looking and all the Children are Above Average."

The 'Men are Toned' phrase helped Cher remember the name of the town she was in: Mentone.

She bought a few things at the Mentone Market and joked with the woman behind the counter about the phrase she had just come up with.

Cher said to her, "This is Mentone – where the Men are Toned… and the Women are Strong, right?"

The woman laughed out loud and said to a local guy sitting at the table. "Ed, did you hear that?"

Ed said quickly, "Yep. And we're Buffed, too." He puffed out his chest.

They all laughed.

He really was Buffed! He had Muscles. And a Tan.

The woman behind the counter added, "Either that or the men are toned deaf."

The 3 of them laughed again.

Cher figured if these people were Funny they must be Smart.

TREA$URE YOUR LIFE | 195

She found out later from the Mentone web site that the name meant:

> *Mentone means 'musical mountain spring' and while natural cascades and rippling streams create a melody all their own, it's the sound of church chimes and harmonizing homefolk that draw the most interest, musically, today.*

How true.

Cher decided to take a chance and see if the money from Mike had already arrived in her checking account. She used her debit card and found out it had! Mike and Sue were very efficient.

After withdrawing $250 from the ATM successfully, she asked the woman behind the counter if there was any Internet service in the area. A Coffee shop? Restaurant? Anything with wireless access?

"Nope. We don't have anything like that here. We don't have any public area with Internet service in Mentone."

Drat. It figured. The town was only two blocks long after all. In the Middle of Nowhere.

The top priority on her list was to get some money from her Scottrade IRA funds. After calling Scottrade back in Minneapolis she found out they needed to fax some forms to her so she could fill it out. Cher asked the woman behind the counter if there was a fax machine in the area.

The woman told her that the only fax machine in town was next door – at the Mentone hardware store.

Great.

Cher took off for the Mentone hardware store and found it was *not exactly* next door.

It was at least a half a mile away. Past many trees. Hundreds of them. Thousands maybe. She didn't count them.

Apparently in small towns the term 'next door' meant the next store after a bunch of trees. A whole forest.

Cher found the Mentone Little River Hardware Store way down the road. It was another place to get local news. She got the forms faxed to her from her Scottrade contact person back in Minneapolis, filled them out and the guy behind the counter at the hardware store faxed them back to Scottrade. No charge.

What??!! No charge? For faxing stuff?

Even in Minneapolis you had to pay to fax stuff everywhere. How did these people make money? Apparently faxing was not their game. Hardware stuff and other cool souvenirs were what they specialized in. They even had fresh vegetables from a local farmer. In a hardware store! Cher had never seen a hardware store that was so versatile.

She bought a few fresh tomatoes and other things.

One was a Cherish picture. It was the word 'Cherish' in a frame that looked awesome. She remembered the song called, Cherish by the Association was Sheridan's favorite song in the whole world.

Sheridan sang often. He knew a lot of songs. During the evening of July 15 after Cher and Sher finished cleaning her sun porch, they took a break. Sher wanted her to play a song on the piano that he could sing. She asked him what his favorite song was.

He told her it was 'Cherish'. He loved that song while he was attending Fridley High School:

> *Cherish is the word I use to describe*
> *All the feeling that I have hiding here for you inside*
>
> *You don't know how many times I've wished that I had told you*
> *You don't know how many times I've wished that I could hold you*
> *You don't know how many times I've wished that I could mold you into someone who could*
> *Cherish me as much as I ... cherish you*
>
> *And I do ... Cherish you*
> *Cherish is the word*

Sheridan sang to her in a wonderful voice. He loved to sing. He sounded like a combination of Johnny Mathis and Elvis Presley. Cher had a music book with the song Cherish in it. She had never played that song before but knew how to read music.

By the time he got to the end of the song Sher could no longer sing because he had tears in his eyes while he was singing to her.

He had to stop. The tears choked him up.

Cher remembered that scene as she was buying the Cherish picture at the Little River Hardware Store in Mentone. She was going to give it to Sher as a souvenir when she got back to Minneapolis.

She also found a black cat picture that she bought for her husband, Michael. They had a black cat named Cezar that Michael was very close to. She figured he'd like it.

She drove back to the Raven Haven Bed and Breakfast. Tony explained to her that breakfast was served every morning at 8:30 am. Cher was free to roam around the gardens on the property during the day.

It was a beautiful set of gardens.

How could I be so lucky as to find this place? I could be dead. If I had killed myself I would never have seen any of this.

This is magical.

She decided to explore. She went from one garden to another in a series of gardens. She wondered who the gardener was. Tony or his wife, Eleanor? She would ask them the next morning at breakfast.

As she was coming back into the house from the kitchen side, she met Eleanor, Tony's wife. And then Cher saw a young girl sitting at the table in the kitchen who was absolutely adorable. She had blond hair and was about 4 years old.

Cher asked the little girl what her name was. The little one said shyly, "Liv."

"That's it? Liv?"

Cher turned to Eleanor who explained that the girl was their Granddaughter. Liv was visiting them for the week. Cher asked if the name "Liv" was short for Olivia.

"Nope", said Eleanor. "It's Liv. That's it. Her parents thought it was a cool name."

"Wow. That's amazing!" Cher had never heard that name before.

Liv reminded Cher of her own daughter, Sarah, at that young age. Both girls were blond-haired, blue-eyed, and precious.

Cher continued to find the little girl absolutely charming. She remembered that during the retreat Edwene had given everybody a set of bubble makers – the kind you blow through to make bubbles. It was so that the seminar participants could have fun during their breaks.

Cher said to little Liv, "I have something for you. I'll be right back."

She went back to her room and got the plastic bubble maker from her suitcase.

Cher gave Liv the bubble maker. They both went outside to make bubbles. Liv was absolutely thrilled with making bubbles!! She blew them all over her Grandmother's gardens. It was like watching a fairy dance around ~ blowing bubbles all over the flowers.

Cher laughed with her. It was great fun.

Cher became known as the Bubble Lady to Liv.

Cher left again to have dinner in town. This time she went across the street from the Wildflower Café to the Moonlight Bistro. She had an exquisite seafood meal outside on the upper deck as the sun was setting.

For a small town these people sure knew how to cook!

After the wonderful dinner she noticed some music from across the main street of Mentone. A block away.

She wandered over to it and discovered an outside private electric flute and guitar concert at The Mentone Inn. People were gathering in the warm summer air to listen to the concert. It was dark.

As Cher was listening to the wonderful music she noticed a field of fireflies in the background. Fireflies???!! She hadn't seen them since she was a little girl back in Minnesota. Where had all the fireflies gone? They were gone from her world, that was for sure.

But the fireflies were still in Mentone, Alabama. Making little white lights all over the field in the background as an electric flutist and guitar player were playing an intimate concert for their Mentone friends. Cher found out later that the 2 musicians were on a national tour. They played the previous night in front of thousands of people.

One of the guys knew the owner of the Mentone Inn and he wanted to do a private special concert. Cher talked to him at the end of the concert. He told her he enjoyed doing the small concerts more than the large crowds because he was so close to people that he felt part of the group. On a big stage it was different.

"How cool was that?" She thought to herself.

Cher got back to her Prairie room around 9 pm and decided to call Mr. Cornbread, her fellow piano player and buddy back in Minneapolis. He was always up late. He enjoyed talking to her. She met Mr. Cornbread at the Dakota club in Minneapolis several years before.

He was an 84 yr old blues piano player who had magic fingers. Cher was fascinated with his performance on a night she was invited to hear another band at the Dakota. Cornbread was the warmup entertainer during Happy Hour. Cher found him more entertaining than the main act that night.

Cher couldn't take her eyes off his black fingers. How did those curled fingers play notes like that? They moved so fast! He didn't even have music in front of him. He played intuitively. From his heart.

After he finished his Happy Hour set that night so many years before, Cher went up to him and introduced herself. She had no idea who he was.

When he told her his name was Cornbread, she said, "Cornbread? That's it?"

He went on to tell her what his real name was – "James Samuel Cornbread Harris, SENIOR", with an emphasis on the word SENIOR.

Cher explained that she was also a piano player. She asked him if he could teach her how to play the piano like him.

He looked up at her warily that night and said, "Maybe."

She got his card and she gave her piano playing card to Cornbread. She asked when she could call him. He told her the next day.

"What time?" She asked.

"Not until after Noon."

She called him the next day at 1 minute after Noon. He answered the phone and they arranged a time for Cher's first lesson. She learned more about chord combinations on the piano than she learned anywhere else. The blues 7th chords, the minor chords, the 9th and 13th notes. It all made sense to her after years of playing the piano.

Cornbread was special. Not only did he teach her chord combinations over a period of time, he listened to her whenever she called him. She was no longer taking lessons from him while she was unemployed – but she could call him at any time as long as it was after Noon.

At least 1 minute after Noon.

She found out that he had a son named Jimmy Jam who grew up knowing another guy named Prince from Minneapolis. Both Prince and Jimmy Jam had moved onto other places. Cornbread was instrumental in their young music careers.

Cornbread stayed in Minneapolis and was still performing in clubs playing the blues piano. At 84! He was amazing.

He called her 'Miss Volleyball' because of her last name. To which she would always respond, 'Oh, Mr. Cornbread.' He always laughed when she said that.

She told Mr. Cornbread she was in Alabama. He was *not* surprised. Cher called Cornbread the few times she traveled around the country and he was never surprised at where she was. Texas, Florida, Chicago, New Orleans. Now Alabama.

She explained what happened on July 15 and how her life had changed dramatically. How she went from almost doing herself in and ending her life to cleaning the sun porch. How Sheridan's last words of 'Just do One Thing ~ Anything' helped her get started. How the entire experience of being successful again at something gave her Hope.

Cornbread knew who Sheridan was from the few times Sher had come with her to piano lessons at Cornbread's house in

Minneapolis. Cornbread also knew about her stressful situation with Michael.

He met Michael one night when Cher and Michael went out to dinner at the Loring Pasta Bar in Dinkytown near the University of Minnesota. Cornbread was playing that night on stage. As he did every Friday night at 84 years old. He played New Orleans style jazz music with a small band. A saxophone player, guitar player, bass and drummer.

On the phone from her Prairie Room in Alabama, Cher confided that she was thinking of ending her marriage. Although there were many good parts to the marriage, Michael's rage and anger were getting to be too much for her.

She also felt worthless as a wife next to Michael's emotional involvement with Angie. There was no sex with Angie, just emotional attachment on his part.

Cornbread listened patiently and offered advice when she asked for it. Cornbread gave her philosophical advice about how to not let life get her so down that she would even consider ending it. He also cautioned her in not leaving a marriage if there was any hope at all.

He was like a Father to her.

At 84 Cornbread was close to her Father's age. He was only 4 years off.

Mr. Cornbread and Miss Volleyball had a wonderful conversation for over an hour. He told her to keep him posted while she was in Alabama. She promised him she would.

She fell asleep again exhausted for a 5th day.

When she woke up the next morning at 5 am her first thought was of the little girl, Liv she'd met the day before. How precious she was. How innocent. How happy Liv was that Cher gave her the bubble maker.

Then, it hit her.

If I hadn't decided to Live, I never would have met Liv!

Cher started crying. It was 5 am in the morning. Who could she call at that hour?

Her buddy, Sher.

She knew Sheridan would be up. That's what time they usually called each other before going to the club every morning. Katherine, his girlfriend, was used to that routine. Sher was awake to Cher's phone call every morning. Or Sher called Cher who was also awake. Whoever was up first called the other one.

He answered his cell phone on the first ring. He was wide awake and could tell it was her calling. "How's it going down there, Cher?"

She was sobbing.

"What's wrong?" He asked.

She told him about the little girl she met the day before and how different her life had become. How she appreciated *everything* these days. How she was really learning how to Live. And Trea$ure her Life.

"Sher, if I had decided *not* to Live, I never would have *met* Liv!!"

Liv would *not* have danced around her grandmother's garden blowing bubbles the day before because Cher wouldn't have been there to give her the bubble maker. Liv wouldn't have made both Cher and her Grandmother laugh.

The innocence of a little girl dancing around beautiful flowers *would not* have caused both women to stop and really enjoy Life. On a beautiful sunny day. For a Moment.

It was a small thing but at the same time a significant event to Cher.

Sheridan got it immediately. He understood.

Thank God for 2nd chances!

Chapter 13 ~ Leaving Mentone

Cher thoroughly enjoyed her time in Mentone. She loved exploring the countryside and venturing into Georgia by mistake. She was only 3 miles from the Georgia state border in the Northeastern corner of Alabama so there were multiple ways of crossing the border to the East and winding up in another state.

The roads changed slightly as she crossed the borders from Alabama to Georgia and back again. She had great fun getting lost on the country roads and then asking local folks the following question:

"Hi. I'm *really* lost. And I'm from Minnesota. Can you tell me how to get back to Minneapolis?"

"What?!" They would say. "Wher ya' from?? Minnesota?"

After she got blank stares while the local folks tried to comprehend just how lost she was, she'd keep a straight face as long as she could but eventually would always burst out laughing.

The looks on their faces were priceless as they tried to imagine where Minnesota or Minneapolis was from their Southern location. She could just as well have been from Mars.

"I'm just kidding. I really *am* lost but need to find out how to get back to Mentone, Alabama. Where the Men are Toned and the Women are Strong. Can you tell me where that is?"

"Oh! Mentone?" - they would reply in their Southern drawl – "You jus' tayk a raht after the next layft and keep goin' till you get to that squiggly lahn on the road. Then you tayk anutha raht to the flashin lahts…"

People sure talk funny down here, she told herself.

She spent time walking around the beautiful gardens of the Raven Haven Bed and Breakfast. She found out both Eleanor and Tony were the gardeners behind it all. They worked well together. They helped each other design the gardens, move plants around and create individual garden areas.

It occurred to her that she and Michael did *not* work so well together on projects. Cher was the gardener at her house. Whenever she did a project that involved tools or building stuff with Michael they almost always got into arguments. She could never seem to do anything right according to him.

Over the course of their 20 year marriage, Cher worked outside in the garden and Michael worked inside.

It was easier that way. Less arguments. Less stress.

Cher was enjoying herself so much that Wednesday morning she asked Eleanor if there was yet another bed and breakfast in the area she could stay at after Wednesday night. The Raven Haven was booked solid for 2 weeks starting on Thursday.

Eleanor called a close friend who also ran a bed and breakfast called The Crystal Lake Lodge. Her friend had one room available for a single night, Thursday. She was booked solid for 2 weeks after that.

"I'll take it!" said Cher. This again, was not part of the Plan. She'd deal with both her Father and her Husband later.

Confident that she had at least until Friday to enjoy Mentone she took off for the Mentone Market to get some groceries. She ran into a woman who was at Edwene's retreat. They recognized each other.

The other woman was surprised to see Cher still in Alabama because Cher told everybody at the end of the retreat she was heading back to Minnesota the next day.

It was fun to run into somebody she recognized. The woman asked Cher if she was going to Edwene's Forgiveness Circle that Wednesday night.

"Oh, I forgot about that," replied Cher.

Actually it's not that she forgot about it, she never really listened to the details of the announcement from Edwene because she figured she'd be back in Minnesota by then. When Cher was reminded that it was open to those who attended the retreat and any other local people who knew about it, she decided to go.

What else was she going to do on a Wednesday night in Mentone?

Cher was happy to be seeing Edwene. She had a feeling she'd see Edwene again in her lifetime but had not expected it to be so soon. She left the Raven Haven in plenty of time Wednesday afternoon to see her favorite Donkey. He was waiting by the fence as she drove by on the dirt road.

He called out "BRAUGGH UHHH" as she pulled up to him. She had carrots for him and stroked his beautiful head. His eyes lit up his whole face. She laughed.

"Mr. Donkey. Did you miss me?"

She still could not believe she was talking to a donkey. What was up with that? Had she totally lost her mind?

She arrived at Edwene's retreat center in Valley Head in plenty of Time. It was The Head of a Valley. Or something like that. That's how she was able to remember the name of it.

Edwene was *not* surprised to see Cher still in Alabama. Cher wondered about that but didn't say anything. Cher told Edwene what happened as she was leaving Monday morning after the retreat and how she suddenly decided to stay longer. Everything fell into place once she started trusting herself and God. And started paying attention to everything around her.

Walking on coals Sunday night had helped.

She was no longer afraid!

The Forgiveness Circle was a major turning point in the healing Cher experienced. Most people in the circle she had never met. She was able to meet John, who both Tony and her husband Michael knew and who was a friend of Robert Bly.

Edwene explained what forgiveness was all about and how each person should focus on one person in their life that they wanted to forgive.

They were encouraged to pick someone they felt had hurt them the *most*.

Cher decided to focus on Tari, her former boss at the University. The one who laid her off. The one she kept trying to forgive but underneath it all still felt hurt by the layoff. The one who had lied to her in a meeting about there *not* being any layoffs during the Budget Crisis, and 5 days later laid her off.

The one who arranged to have her walked out the door without giving her a chance to say goodbye to anyone ~ even to her own PeopleSoft team.

Tari was the one who tried to prove Cher did *not* have enough seniority in her position as PeopleSoft Manager by taking out the lines in her re-hire letter that said she was fully reinstated.

Tari could *not* manage a team of web programmers successfully. She was the one who had no college degree and yet had been appointed to a Director position within the University…. in what Cher called a Freak Reorg where nothing made sense.

Cher wasn't told about the reorganization by Rod *before* it happened. As a manager that was one of the traditions within the University community. Managers were told ahead of time. It allowed them to be ready for questions from their staff. But not in a Freak Reorg.

In fact, Cher found out she had a new boss when one of her Payroll team members told her right before their regular 8 am PeopleSoft checkpoint meeting started, "So now you're reporting to Tari?! How do you feel about that?"

"WHAT????!!! What are you talking about?!!" She thought Jim was kidding. He had been known to play jokes on people. Just like Cher.

But Jim was not joking. Cher didn't think it was Funny.

The email from Rod telling the entire department of the reorganization which suddenly put Tari in charge of 100 people had been sent out just a few minutes before 8 am. Cher was busy getting ready for the 8 am meeting and never saw it.

That's how unprofessional the Freak Reorg was. Informing managers in an email to the *whole department* their new boss was Tari instead of calling a private meeting ahead of time. It was completely out of the ordinary! Was Rod worried about their reaction to that?? To Tari being the new 'boss'? Did he not want to see the look on their faces when he told them?

Tari was the one who was told by Marilyn from HR that she had to be more like Cher because Tari was so chaotic. And 2 weeks later Tari became Cher's boss.

It was difficult for Cher to imagine Tari in her thoughts, even after all she had gone through ~ she was still hurt. But after an hour-long session with Edwene guiding the group, Cher's thoughts turned to Forgiveness.

Cher found herself saying silently:

> "If Tari hadn't laid me off, I wouldn't be in such a beautiful place. I wouldn't have come close to ending my life and then truly appreciating it. I wouldn't have noticed Dragonflies or Donkeys or Fireflies. I wouldn't have seen the Moon over the Chattanooga Valley while listening to angelic music on the radio.
>
> I would never have heard Tree Frogs that sound like exotic birds. I wouldn't have walked on fire without getting hurt. I would not have met a dancing little girl named Liv who had fun with bubbles.
>
> I would never have been blessed by this wonderful woman named Edwene. Did that really happen? She

believes in me. But then, she believes in a *lot* of people. There is something about Edwene's presence that is very gratifying.

Tari, I forgive you. You have given me so much more awareness. I truly appreciate my Life like I never had before. It is a gift to be here in Alabama and in this beautiful retreat place. I would not have been here if you hadn't laid me off. I really Trea$ure my Life.

Thank you."

Cher felt a tremendous lightness. She had tears in her eyes. She was free! Her thoughts of regret and anger were gone! This was her Life now and she was going to appreciate every Moment.

Edwene explained that Forgiveness allowed one to move forward and not be stuck in the past anymore. You were no longer a prisoner to your own anger.

Cheryl remembered reading on her Unity church web site:

> *"Forgiveness is unlocking the door to set someone free and... realizing you were the prisoner!"*
> - Max Lucado

After the Forgiveness Circle ended, Cher was talking with the woman who invited her and explaining that she was trying to stay in Mentone as long as possible but did not know where to stay after Thursday night. She was given the names of two other women who might have places to stay.

The first woman was named Terri ~ the same name as her former boss but with a different spelling.

Another Tari!!

Cher had no problem with that name anymore. From the time of her layoff and up until the Forgiveness Circle every time she heard the name Tari for a woman she felt as if somebody had punched her in the stomach. She got tense. It actually hurt. She would become angry.

But now the hurt was gone. She knew her forgiveness exercise had paid off.

She called Terri and arranged to stay through Sunday of the weekend. Cher was excited. She didn't have to go back to Minnesota yet and face her Husband!

A woman whose named sounded like Tari had come through for her by providing her with a place to stay in a strange town. Instead of a woman named Tari trying to hurt her.

Whoo-Hoo~!!

And the original Tari? Did she have any idea what Cher had gone through all those 8 years? How she had come very close to suicide due to an unwarranted layoff?

Nope. She probably didn't feel a thing. Why was Cher torturing herself for years with anger and hurt towards a woman who was *not at all hurt* by what she had done??!

The pain was gone.

Life was good.

On Thursday morning she was getting ready to leave the Raven Haven for her next place. After having another wonderful home-cooked breakfast by Tony, Eleanor pulled her aside.

She said, "Liv has something for you. She's never done this before with any of our guests."

"What is it?" Cher asked.

Liv came forward and shyly presented Cher with an embroidered white angel 3 inches long and 2 inches wide. It was precious.

"Wow!" Said Cher. "Thanks, Liv. Where did you get this?"

The little girl replied shyly and in a small voice, "My Grandmother made it but *you* can have it."

Eleanor explained the angel was a Christmas ornament that was hand-made and embroidered but Liv had asked her grandmother if she could give it to The Bubble Lady.

Cher was really touched by this. *The Bubble Lady?* Is that what Liv called her? Liv had never given a gift before to any of their guests. An angel. How cool was that?

Cher put the angel carefully in her hand and said goodbye to them all. When she got into the car, she put the angel on the console of her Toyota Corolla so that she could see it at all times while driving.

She arrived at The Crystal Lake Lodge at 10 am. Exactly on Time.

Claudia, the hostess of the bed and breakfast opened the door to greet her and said with surprise, "Oh My God. You're ON TIME!" To which Cher wondered to herself, What was up with that?

Claudia added, "Nobody around here is *ever* on Time!"

"Oh then, I should fit right in," replied Cher.

Claudia introduced herself and her husband Dave, and then opened the door. Cher looked into a large beautiful family room with a fireplace and a high ceiling. She was taken to the only bedroom they had available: The Forest Room.

It figured. She was from Minnesota after all. The whole trees and prairie theme seemed to be occurring in different places she was staying.

The bedroom she was taken to had a high ceiling with large windows looking out over the expansive back yard next to some woods. As she made her way to the bathroom she was delighted to find it had a waterfall over a log frame creating the shower. The bathroom was painted as if it was a forest of trees.

Enchanting.

"This is so cool! I have to call Sher and tell him about it."

Why she chose *not* to call her husband, Michael, she didn't really know. It could have been that Michael seemed always busy and somewhat annoyed whenever she would call, as if she were interrupting him. Which of course, she was. Any phone call interrupts the caller.

She remembered how Michael wasn't annoyed the few times Angie called him. In fact, he was overjoyed.

But Sheridan was *never* annoyed when she called him. Any time of day or night. He always seemed to be happy when she called him.

"Sher, you wouldn't believe the shower in this place!! It looks like a waterfall in the woods! The ceiling must be 10 feet high! I've never seen anything like it! It is so cool that I wish I could show it to you!!"

He laughed at her excitement.

He was one person who gave her support for her journey to Alabama and for staying longer to experience it. He didn't question it. In fact, he even continued offering his support by saying, "Maybe you should think about moving down there ~ you seem to like it so much."

Cher replied with, "Oh, I couldn't do that right now. But it sure is nice to be in a place where I have Time to think about things. Without getting into arguments with Michael over stuff. I'm away from his underlying Anger. This is really helping me sort through things."

She asked him how his workouts were going at Bally's. He admitted that he hadn't worked out since she left. He was sleeping in every morning and trying to organize stuff in his world and in Katherine's. He had gotten into the habit of *not* working out at all while Cher was gone.

Sheridan wasn't going to the club without her.

She wondered about that. After they hung up, her mind flashed back to when she first met him.

She remembered how working out every morning was part of *his* world when they met each other. They both were early morning people and would arrive at Bally's shortly after 5 am each morning when the club opened. They met 10 years before while soaking in the hot tub one morning on the 1st floor of Bally's. In the pool area.

He started the conversation with her that fateful morning by stretching out his arms along the top of the hot tub and saying, "Hi my name's Sher."

His arm stretch took up half the pool, she noticed. At least 6 feet of it anyway.

To which she replied, "How can *that* be? *My name* is Cher, too!"

The both looked at each other in astonishment. Another Sher/Cher?

He admitted that his real name was Sheridan but had been called 'Sher' since he was a teenager. She told him her real name was Cheryl but had been called 'Cher' by her family since she was a teenager.

Even *before* there was *another Cher*.

Many years later they discovered they were the same age. Only 4 months apart from each other. She was older.

Their relationship took a different turn from the occasional meetings in the hot tub to a more consistent meeting one morning when Sheridan crawled up the stairs to the 2nd floor of the Bally's workout center to find Cheryl stretching out before a run. It was 5:15 AM.

"So what do people do up here?" he asked her.

She laughed and said, "What are *you* doing up here? I only see you downstairs in the pool area."

He explained that he was on a new program to lose weight. His Vietnamese girlfriend was in Vietnam for two months and he was trying to lose 20 pounds before she got back. Swimming wasn't doing it for him anymore. He needed something more than that.

Cher told him, "Well, I used to be a Personal Trainer here at Bally's so I know a few things about the equipment up here. I could show you some stuff.

First of all you have to know the definition of **Exercise: Running when nobody is chasing you and lifting things that don't need to be lifted.**"

She remembered him laughing at that.

It was the start of their working out together every morning at 5:15 am. She had a Husband. He had a Girlfriend. There was no intent to impress or flirt with each other. They weren't at the club to meet anybody. They were at the club to stay in shape. They both loved going to the club and working out every morning.

On their own.

At 5 am.

The morning he crawled up the stairs to the 2nd floor was Cher's birthday. On a Monday in March. Because it was her birthday, she asked him when *his* birthday was.

His birthday was in July. *Of the same year.*

That's when she found out how old he was. They were only 4 months apart.

They started meeting at the club every morning after that so Cher could help him learn all the machines in order to lose weight for his Vietnamese girlfriend.

He did lose almost 20 pounds. He also lost his girlfriend.

He discovered when his girlfriend came back from Vietnam after two months that they had many communication problems. One of them was a language barrier that he had been trying to deal with for a couple of years but had been overlooking. She had a Vietnamese accent that made her very difficult to understand. He was very patient.

The other issue they had was that she was extremely jealous of any female he looked at or talked to. He noticed it the first time they went to Vietnam to visit her relatives. He said a few things to the woman seated next to her on the plane and for the next 13 hours on the flight was berated by his girlfriend for even talking to the total stranger.

Sheridan broke up with his girlfriend a few months after she came back from Vietnam. She couldn't handle the fact he was working out every morning with another woman. A woman named Cher.

And he realized he could no longer deal with their language barriers. Or her control issues. Or her constantly repeating things as if she was in a never-ending loop.

He quickly found another girlfriend. And another. Katherine was one of a series of women he hooked up with who he tried to help.

Katherine was the one he was living with when Cher went on her journey to Alabama. And Katherine's mess was what he was trying to clean up while Cher was gone, in addition to his own mess in the garage.

It was an effort that would ultimately end in disaster. He just didn't know it yet.

What Sheridan found out and Cheryl did too, is that you cannot clean up somebody else's mess or change them. You can only work on yourself. It's that simple.

The realization Cher had that morning in Alabama was that if Tari hadn't laid her off at the University of Minnesota, she never would have pursued and become a Personal Fitness Trainer at Bally's.

She had been working out at Bally's every day before going to her job as an Information Technology Manager at the University. She just had to take some training and past some certification tests in order to become a Personal Fitness Trainer professionally.

Which she did.

She studied hard and passed the written tests on her first try. She was warned by Bally's staff that it might take several attempts to pass the tests. Just like she was warned by several people that it would take many attempts to get into the Carlson School of Management, but she got accepted on her first application.

She figured she was lucky.

Cher also rediscovered her love at playing the piano due to her sudden layoff. She took an unemployment workshop and was encouraged to focus on an area in her life where she was young and playing around. Just playing. At anything.

During the unemployment workshop she realized that playing the piano was a very large part of her life growing up. She decided to pursue piano playing as one avenue of making money.

Cher was surprised at the amount of money people would pay her for playing the piano after her layoff. For her, playing the piano was easy. It was like playing in a sandbox as a little kid.

If Tari hadn't laid her off she never would have met Mike Paxton, the CEO who she gave piano lessons to for many years. Mike was now a good friend of hers and helped her stay in Alabama for a few more days ~ so she could experience the Forgiveness Circle.

She wouldn't have met Mike because she wouldn't have met Anastasia, a consultant who was a leader of a networking group for unemployed women. Anastasia introduced her to Mike. Anastasia was also a good friend of hers now, too.

She wouldn't have met Anastasia because Cher would never have attended a meeting for unemployed women through the State of Minnesota's unemployment program.

She also wouldn't have taught piano lessons to the children of another CEO in the Minneapolis area and gotten to know him. His name was Gary Bhojwani and he worked for a company called Allianz, an international organization with a North American headquarters in Minneapolis.

She was referred to Gary's wife by the parents of other kids in Gary's neighborhood that she was teaching. Due to her layoff she started teaching piano and found she loved doing it.

She pondered all this from her bed and breakfast in Mentone at the Crystal Lake Lodge.

If Tari hadn't laid her off she never would have met Mr. Cornbread who was another close friend of hers and a piano player. She wouldn't have been at the Dakota night club in Minneapolis due to her connections in the music world after her layoff.

She wouldn't have had a business card to hand to him at the Dakota night club in Minneapolis that indicated she was a Project Manager *and Piano Player*. She wouldn't have taken blues lessons from him and gotten to know him personally.

Cornbread Harris was the father of Jimmy Jam Harris and friend of Prince, all who were from Minneapolis. Cornbread taught her more about blues chords than anyone she knew.

Cher also realized from her stay in Mentone that if Tari hadn't laid her off she never would have built a website for her classical piano teacher, Tadeusz Majewski.

Tadeusz, her classical piano teacher grew up in Poland studying Chopin and became famous enough to travel throughout the United States giving concerts by the time he was 19 years old.

Cher met Tadeusz through one of her husband's guy friends who had a new girlfriend, Liz Lupien. Liz was a piano player and student of Tadeusz.

Cher remembered the party she was at when she met Liz. They were talking about playing the piano. Liz told her she was taking piano lessons and the first thought Cher had was, "Aren't you too OLD to be taking piano lessons?" She thought those words but didn't say them. She realized she was the same age as Liz.

After getting introduced to Tadeusz at one of Liz's dinner parties, she was fascinated with his piano playing. She found out he was a concert pianist and had played with various orchestras including the Minnesota Symphony Orchestra.

Liz told Cher she would have to audition to be one of Tadeusz' students. Cher auditioned and got in to his circle of adult students. Cher realized in her middle age that one is never too OLD to take piano lessons. There is always more to learn. One thing she learned from Tadeusz was how to play classical music very passionately. Not mechanically, as many did.

When Cher got laid off by Tari she had already been taking lessons from Tadeusz in his Minneapolis home for a few years. He agreed to continue giving her lessons for free if she built him a website. After her layoff she couldn't afford to pay him. He needed a website and she needed to continue taking piano lessons from him to exercise her brain.

They worked out an arrangement. Through the U of M Computer Center's short courses Cher was able to figure out how to scan his CD photos, crop them using Photoshop, build a website with Dreamweaver and allow people to buy his CD's online by contacting him.

She set him up with a domain name through her husband's company and proceeded to design Tadeusz' website. She learned how to build Tadeusz's website because of two year's worth of free short courses she was offered as part of her U of M settlement after she won the layoff grievance.

She wondered if Stanley had anything to do with that part (offering free short courses). He must have known how much she loved to learn. Tari and Rod certainly wouldn't have known. Nor would they have cared.

Instead of being angry and hurt, she was now grateful for the things she had in her life.

She had gotten some free website and HTML training ~ enough to figure out how to do stuff on the web.

If she hadn't gotten laid off from Tari, she never would have learned how to arrange flowers professionally. After her layoff, she

224 | TREA$URE YOUR LIFE

got a part-time job at a local florist shop called Riverside Florist owned by her friend, Linnea, near the Mississippi River.

She learned a lot about arranging flowers from Linnea. She used this to entertain friends. It came in handy and saved her money in the long run.

Arranging flowers was becoming her passion. She was arranging flowers for everybody now ~ mostly wild flowers from alongside the road. People loved the bouquets she made for them. She pondered this from her bed and breakfast in Alabama.

She was loving Life!

If Tari hadn't laid her off from the University of Minnesota, Cher never would have traveled all the way to Alabama and met the wonderful Edwene Gaines. Cher realized that her Karate Kid Master was Edwene. The Master Edwene taught her how to deal with Bullying Women by creating Goals, using Words to heal from the hurting behavior and applying Love and Forgiveness to move on.

Cher appreciated her life at the University *even more* when she was hired back after being gone for 2 years. The camaraderie, the close network of friends, the continuous learning atmosphere, the cutting edge technology of working with Smart people... ALL of it she treasured more the 2nd time around!

And when her job was taken away from her suddenly and without warning ~ it caused her tremendous feelings of total devastation. Life had no meaning after that.

But if she hadn't gotten laid off by Tari she wouldn't have known what it was like to lose focus on life, jobs, and everything that mattered. And then find out what is truly important in Life. How precious Life truly is.

How quickly Life can be taken away never to return. How we really don't get a 2nd chance if we end it.

Our life is not a movie that can be re-done with different outcomes.

She decided to call Sally, her best friend from high school who lived in California and tell her what was happening. She had been updating Sally periodically but finally had a chance to go into detail about the trip to Alabama and the situation with Michael.

Sally, as usual, listened intently.

Sally said, "I'm shocked, Cheri, that you had to go through all of this! But glad you made the right decision *not* to end your life."

Cher could tell by the tone of Sally's voice that she was very concerned. They had known each other over 40 years.

"I'm all right now, Sal, don't worry about me. Everything is going to be all right. Tell my Neighbor I said Hi."

Cher's Neighbor was Sally's Husband. The Cute Guy Next Door that Cher had grown up with. And known since she was 3 years old. His name was Greg. She still called him Neighbor. Greg called her Neighbor, too.

Cher spent the rest of the week enjoying the various places she stayed at. She looked at each day and every event as a new experience. One to be Trea$ured. She took lots of pictures ~ often of Dragonflies.

She studied one Dragonfly for 30 minutes Friday morning on the dock of the Crystal Lake Lodge overlooking a small lake as the sun rose over the lake. The morning mist was captivating. Actually it was breath-taking against a calm, still lake.

She thought the Dragonfly was dead on the dock. She knelt down beside it and looked at it intently before she noticed that its *legs were moving*! That's all that was moving to prove it was alive. The legs were so tiny. Its two front legs were rubbing together like tiny hands getting ready to do something.

What a concept! It took intensity and patience for her to realize that.

Again, if she were dead she never would have seen it!

She would have been a Spirit somewhere, if Spirits exist, regretting the fact she took her own life. She would *not* have been given a 2nd chance. She would *not* have seen something as simple as a Dragonfly moving its legs on a warm August morning in Alabama.

It was another revelation for her. Life in all forms was truly precious! Even tiny Dragonflies.

She was really getting it.

She was taking pictures of the Dragonfly on the dock around 6 am when Dave, the Proprietor of the Crystal Lake Lodge drove up in his yellow SmartCar. He got out of the car and studied her as she was intently taking pictures of the Dragonfly.

"He must think I'm crazy," she thought.

If he thought that, he didn't say that. She explained that she was taking pictures of a Dragonfly on his dock. He said simply, "Of course you are."

She thought he was Funny which made him Smart.

He took it all in stride. Then he left.

On Friday afternoon she showed up at Terri's house with instructions on where the key was. Terri called to say she was giving a massage at another location and would not be back in time to let Cher in to the house.

When Cher got to Terri's house in the woods, she noticed dark blue bottles hanging from tree branches next to the driveway. The dark blue color of the bottles represented her mother's Spirit. It had existed in Cher's world since she had gone on a retreat years before through the Woman Within organization. She felt connected to her mother who had died from a heart attack at age 43.

Every time Cher thought of her mother, the color of deep blue appeared around her. Or if the color of deep blue appeared around her, she thought of her mother, Doris.

As she drove to Terri's house it was thinking about her mother that caused her to notice the blue bottles. Cher started crying. She really missed her mother. It had been over 35 years since she was gone, but the pain of the loss was still there. Her mother became unconscious immediately after having a heart attack so Cher was not able to say goodbye.

Nobody in her family was able to say goodbye. Not even Cher's father.

"Mom, I wish you could see this beautiful place. It's magical and comforting. The people around here are so nice. If only I could talk to you ~ I don't really know what to do about Michael. You've never met him but I think you would have liked him."

Her mother loved Cher's first Husband, John. She was totally supportive of their marriage. She knew John loved her daughter. When Cher's mother died suddenly it was the start of the end of her first marriage. The pain of her mother's loss was too much to handle. John kept telling her to "Get over it." Which didn't help.

Cher still had tears in her eyes while she walking up the path to the door. She started noticing other dark blue stones and dark blue items. She felt her mother was surrounding her in some strange, weird way.

This had happened before. Cher took her time walking around the beautiful house in the woods before trying the key. The more time she spent thinking about her mother, the more she cried.

Shortly afterwards, Terri arrived. Cher was still teary-eyed from the experience. She wound up telling Terri about the Woman Within retreat she had gone on many years before and how she felt closer to her mother's Spirit after that.

Terri was amazed at the story. It brought both women together instantly.

Terri and Cher spent the evening sharing stories and getting to know each other. At the end of the evening Terri invited her back to a Hawaiian luau party the next night. Cher was planning on moving to her last place of stay in Mentone the next morning, at a woman's house named Laura who she'd met during the Forgiveness Circle.

Laura was a close friend of Terri's who was trying to get into the business of having a bed and breakfast. The only problem was that Laura felt her house was not quite ready.

Cher went over to Laura's house Saturday morning to help her clean and organize stuff. Cher laughed when she saw Laura's living room ~ it was cluttered and reminded her of the sun porch. Laura felt overwhelmed.

Laura said, "I'm so sorry about the mess. I just can't get a handle on it."

Cher replied, "Laura, if you could have seen *my house* before I started cleaning it, you would have been *totally* shocked. This place is *nothing* like mine. It just needs a bit of organizing, that's all. Mine was much worse. This doesn't bother me at all to look at."

The two of them worked together to throw things away and clean up before getting ready for the Hawaiian luau party, each driving separately.

Cher left first for the luau party and got to Terri's house by late Saturday afternoon. She was able to help Terri get ready and hand out Hawaiian leis to guests as they arrived.

The phrase they said to each guest *suggestively* was, "You've just been lei'd."

Guests who were paying attention laughed at the phrase.

A handsome guy named John pointed to Cher and said, "I want to get leighed by *her!*"

Great, thought Cher. Another John. Just what I need. I married a guy named John once. I don't need to do *that* again.

Then to herself, she realized that the term getting 'laid' or 'lei'd' or 'lay ed' at this party was another reflection of the term 'layed off'. Suddenly any reference to layoff just made her laugh. She was no longer in pain.

The Forgiveness Circle had been a key to her recovery.

Cher was having fun looking at other men even though she was married. It was something she hadn't done in her 20 years of marriage. She joked with them and enjoyed the conversations. She felt young again. She noticed that some of the men seemed to be interested in her.

What a concept! She hadn't felt that way in many years ~ appreciating the fact that men were finding her interesting and even attractive. She felt her husband, Michael, found her quite boring and plain these days. At least compared to Angie.

Her mind flashed back to when she met Rich. A substitute Postman in her Prospect Park neighborhood. She met him the day after seeing the movie, *'What About Bob?'* with Sheridan. He was a new Postman filling in for their regular guy who was on vacation. Cher was weeding her garden in the front lawn before getting ready to drive to Chicago and then Alabama.

Rich came up the walk and Cher noticed immediately that he was different. He was not Tim, the regular guy. Rich was good-looking and very outgoing. Rich joked with her about what she was doing in the front yard and engaged her in a quick-witted conversation about the *'What About Bob?'* movie.

Cher said things that made Rich laugh. He must have thought she was Funny.

She remembered telling Rich that she was married to Richard Dreyfuss, the Psychiatrist. And that *she* was Bob in the movie. She *was* Bill Murray.

He said, "So, are you going to drive *him* nuts?" He pointed to her house. Implying something about her Husband.

To which she replied, "Maybe."

Ah yes, the fun of flirting, she remembered. With no expectations. She hadn't felt like that since she was a teenager.

At the luau party, her mind flashed back to the different person she had become since July 15.

Even her long-time hairdresser, Andre noticed the change. Before July 15 she had become so difficult and hard to please that Andre refused to cut her hair anymore. He had a charming salon on Grand Ave in St. Paul called the Andre Franca Studio. He ran the business with his sister Franca.

After July 15 Cher made an effort to reconnect with Andre by giving him a bamboo plant and apologizing for being so depressing and difficult. He accepted both her apology and the plant. Then he took her back as a client.

Andre remarked at the sudden change in her. He couldn't believe it. She told him all about her near suicide and like the excellent hairdresser that he was, he listened intently.

The new haircut from Andre before her trip to Alabama helped boost her confidence. She felt somewhat attractive again.

She met a number of other locals at the Hawaiian luau party. They all had stories to tell about why they wound up in the area. The

Northeastern corner of Alabama. The Middle of Nowhere. Most of the stories were spiritual.

Someone at the party told her the area around Mentone had one of the highest natural energy fields on earth. There was a reason so many people from spiritual communities gathered in the area for conferences. There was an unexplained connection between the energy forces of this Life and other life forms.

Cheryl was intrigued.

"So *that could* explain why Robert Bly and Edwene Gaines organize retreats here. I had no idea it was such a high energy area."

She had a wonderful time dancing and meeting other people at the party. Terri had lights on her patio with music playing from a boom box. Towards the end of the night Cher left shortly after Laura did. They both met back at Laura's house and talked about the good time they had.

Laura showed Cher the bedroom she was going to be staying in. It was filled with lots of stuffed pet lambs. Everywhere. Cher had never seen such a collection of stuffed animals that were *all* lambs. They were so Cute.

When Cher was at Laura's house earlier that morning helping her clean, she never noticed the bedroom. They had been focused on cleaning the living room.

Lambs. WHAT THE ---?!!

There was something nagging at her about the scene in Laura's bedroom with all the stuffed pet Lambs, but Cher couldn't put her finger on it. Why lambs?

She fell asleep after talking to Laura for hours. It was as if they were both teenagers who were on a 'sleep-over' with good friends. They seemed to bond instantly. Both of them never had any sisters. The bed was soft and wonderful. Laura slept on the couch in the living room.

Cher woke up the next morning at 4 am before Laura was awake and wandered outside. The sun was not up but the early light was enough for her to see the area. She saw the horizon over a field on Laura's property. She also discovered an amazing garden next to a wooden shed that had signs of remodeling efforts.

In the full moonlight she started weeding the garden. She could tell it had been neglected, much like her own garden after months of depression.

She could relate. A neglected garden often meant the gardener was depressed.

As she pulled each weed, Cher was reminded of her own weeding efforts on the weekend of July 15. A weekend that was an Eternity away from her in Alabama. And yet right around the corner in Real Time. Not that far away. Only one Month. Another Full Moon.

She remembered Laura telling her the night before that she was overwhelmed by her own remodeling efforts. Laura had been neglecting her garden, which she loved. She needed to get the shed remodeled and fixed up so that she could expand her own business ~ a dance and yoga studio.

The dance/yoga studio was nearing completion. The only problem was that the garden next to it was suffering.

Cher noticed in the moonlight that the plants were struggling with the weeds. The weeds were winning. Clearly.

With Cher's weeding help, the beautiful plants Laura planted in the Spring were given a chance at survival. When Laura woke up and wandered outside with some freshly made coffee for Cher, she was shocked.

"Oh my God! How did you do this? When did you get up??!"

"I guess around 4 am. I wasn't paying attention really. I couldn't sleep any longer so I wandered outside."

Laura was inspired by all the weeding Cher had done, so she joined in the effort. Both of them worked silently, slowly weeding the garden together. Cher noticed a particularly large plant with huge white flowers that were similar to a Lily but not quite the same.

Laura explained that it was a Moon plant.

Moon plant?

"What in the world is that?" asked Cher.

Laura said it was a perennial plant that came up on its own. This particular year it was more expansive than normal. It was one of the most beautiful plants Cher had ever seen. The white flower was large and yet exquisite.

Laura offered to dig up a part of the plant and send it back with Cher.

"Really? Can you do that? I could take part of it back to Minnesota?"

"Yes, of course," replied Laura.

A Moon plant, thought Cher. How cool was that? Especially after the Moon had been guiding her on the journey to Alabama.

They worked together to dig up a small section of the plant and put it in a box so Cher could take it back to Minnesota. Then they added water to a plastic pot base for the long trip.

It was Sunday morning. Cher was planning on starting her drive back to Minnesota that day. She was finally ready to go back. The Forgiveness Circle from Edwene was the turning point for her.

Cher mentioned to Laura that she wanted to go to church first. The only church Cher knew was the St. Whatever on the Mountain church in Mentone.

Laura looked pensive.

"Really? You want to go there??" asked Laura.

"Yes," said Cher. "It's the only church around here that means anything to me."

To which Laura replied, "Well, you go on without me. I don't think I could go there with you. I'll go *anywhere* but there."
Hmmm…. thought Cher.

"Why not?"

Laura replied, "The last time I went to that church was for the funeral of a dear friend. She committed suicide. She hung herself with a rope in her garage. Her grown son found her there. We all knew she was depressed for a long time but didn't know how to help her. I felt guilty for not calling her often enough."

Cher was stunned. Another suicide. And a *hanging* suicide at that. Cher had experienced that before with people in her life. Twice.

"Maybe if you went there you could start healing from your friend's suicide," Cher offered.

Laura gave it some thought. "Maybe…" was all she said.

After several minutes of silently weeding the garden, Laura finally said, "OK. I'm going with you."

"Are you kidding me? WHOA ~ Awesome!" said Cher.

Cher figured it wouldn't hurt if they drove to the church together. After all, Cher was under no Time schedule. Even though she was planning on leaving that day she did not have a specific time. She just needed to get back home eventually.

She was finally ready to leave and face her Husband in Minneapolis.

And her Father in Chicago.

They decided to stop weeding and get ready for church.

Cher and Laura arrived a few minutes late for the service at St Joseph's on the Mountain Episcopal Church. Cher noted it was about 5 minutes too late. Because they were late, there were no seats left in the church. Except at the front.

"Great. Just like a Lutheran church," thought Cheryl. "Nobody wants to sit in the front row."

Followed by thoughts of, "I really HATE being late. I wish we hadn't weeded so long."

TREA$URE YOUR LIFE

They were forced to sit in the very front row of the small church on the left side. Cher felt as if everyone knew everybody else and that they were all looking at her. After a few minutes she calmed down and was able to look at the inside of the church.

It was beautiful. Lots of wood carvings and stained glass. It had the look and feel of a 100 year old church. At the front of the altar was a huge picture of a Lamb. An innocent Lamb looking out at everybody in the congregation.

A Lamb. It was at least 10 feet high. Cher was stunned at both the size of the Lamb and the fact it was the only thing to the right of the altar. No picture of Jesus or Mary or Joseph or anybody else from the Bible.

Just a Lamb.

Oh My God, OMG! The Lamb of God. Of course!

Maybe this was the church Cher was supposed to find in Mentone, with the references to Lamb of God on the radio as she drove down there?

What the ---?!! But why?

Was it to bring Laura to this church again so that she could get over her friend's suicide and finally move on? Laura had a Lamb collection, of all things!!

No, it couldn't be that. Or could it?

Cher's heart was racing as she sat in the church trying to make sense of everything around her as if she were putting the pieces together of an enormous jigsaw puzzle. She loved putting puzzles together.

It was one of the ways she made sense out of lots of data. Her daughter Sarah was also excellent at putting together jigsaw puzzles. That thought crossed her mind in the church.

She found herself drifting in and out of the sermon. She couldn't really focus on anything. There was too much data to process.

Laura seemed to be listening intently.

Finally Cher's mind was able to focus on the Moment. She heard the pastor talk about Forgiveness. Letting go of the past. Letting go of regret. Forgiving someone else's mistakes. Even forgiving our own failures.

Letting go of our guilt in situations of suicides of friends or family members.

What? Did she hear that right?!

Letting go of *our guilt* in suicide situations of friends or family members? Forgiving *our own* failures?

Cher had her own history with dealing in the aftermath of suicides. Successful ones. Ones where the people actually followed through and ended their lives. It was painful to be a survivor.

Emotionally painful. Especially if you were related to the ones who ended their lives.

Why would anybody want to do that to those around them?

And then she REALLY got it! She was at the brink of suicide only a month before. Ready to end her life without looking back.

READY to MOVE on into the next world!!

But then she stopped, and asked herself,

And THEN what?...

ENDNOTES

[1] McLean and Elkind, *The Smartest Guys in the Room,* (New York: Penguin Group, 2003, rev. 2013), 132.

[2] Ibid, 3-4.

[3] Ibid, 119.

[4] Ibid, 428.